P9-BZI-971

WITH LIBERTY FOR ALL

SWAN LIBRARY
BECKER COLLEGE-LEICESTER, MA

Other books by the author

Books edited by the author

WITH LIBERTY FOR ALL

FREEDOM OF RELIGION
IN THE UNITED STATES

Phillip E. Hammond

Westminster John Knox Press
Louisville, Kentucky

© 1998 Phillip E. Hammond

All rights reserved.
No part of this book may be reproduced or
transmitted in any form or by any means, electronic or mechanical,
including photocopying, recording, or by any information storage or
retrieval system, without permission in writing from the publisher.
For information, address Westminster John Knox Press,
100 Witherspoon Street, Louisville, Kentucky 40202-1396.

Book and cover design by Jennifer K. Cox
Cover photography by Richard Berenholtz,
courtesy of The Stock Market®.

First edition
Published by Westminster John Knox Press
Louisville, Kentucky

This book is printed on acid-free paper that meets the
American National Standards Institute Z39.48 standard. ∞

PRINTED IN THE UNITED STATES OF AMERICA
98 99 00 01 02 03 04 05 06 07 — 10 9 8 7 6 5 4 3 2 1

Library of Congress Cataloging-in-Publication Data

Hammond, Phillip E.
    With liberty for all : freedom of religion in the Unted States /
Phillip E. Hammond.
        p.   cm.
    Includes bibliographical references and index.
    ISBN 0-664-25768-2
    1. Freedom of religion—United States.   2. United States—
Religion.   I. Title
BR516.H2   1998
323.44′2′0973—dc21   97-28819

DEDICATED TO THE STUDENTS
IN RELIGIOUS STUDIES 141C

CONTENTS

PREFACE

While not a lengthy product, this work is the outgrowth of a lengthy period in my teaching. One of the great advantages of moving to the University of California at Santa Barbara after eighteen years in sociology departments was my freedom to teach a variety of courses in the sociology of religion. One of these is subtitled "Church and State," and over the years at UCSB it has attracted a great many serious and intelligent students. This manuscript reflects my engagement with that course. While my interest in the topic goes back to my days as a graduate student, I am sure I would not have done the sustained reading and thinking required for this book had it not been for Religious Studies 141C.

I benefited enormously from the close reading of the first draft by two colleagues, Professor Laura Kalman of UCSB's History Department and Professor Ronald B. Flowers of the Religious Studies Department of Texas Christian University. Kalman holds both a law degree and a Ph.D. in history, while Flowers is a long-time published scholar in the church-state field. Their affirmative response to my efforts gave me a boost in confidence, though of course they cannot be held responsible for any places herein where that confidence proves ill founded.

I acknowledge, too, the assistance in several ways of Eric M. Mazur, now a faculty member at Bucknell University. From the time he began graduate study at UCSB, he has been a valuable source of ideas, data gathering, and fun. He, too, read my manuscript. Collaborator with me on several projects, Eric was one of those students who make academic life so rewarding.

Finally, I must acknowledge the passion with which I wrote. There is clearly a concerted effort to undo what has to be one of America's greatest accomplishments—the near absence of religious strife in our public life. This effort must be defeated. Since most academic publishing is dispassionate, perhaps that means this book is not academic. So be it.

INTRODUCTION

In a review of *Church and State in the United States* by Anson Phelps Stokes, Mark DeWolfe Howe wrote (1950:172):

The political conviction that religious liberty is of profound importance generally bespeaks at least a Protestant, and very frequently a skeptical, attitude towards the "truths" of religion. Behind our constitutional provisions there may lie, therefore, an attitude towards religion, if not a religious faith itself, which is predominantly Protestant in spirit.

Professor Howe's comments were designed less to characterize Protestantism than to give context to his criticism of Canon Stokes for minimizing, in his monumental survey of American church-state history, the truly revolutionary implications of the Religion Clauses of the Constitution's First Amendment. The Framers, Howe asserted, aimed at "converting the liberal principle of tolerance into the radical principle of liberty" by prohibiting the governmental establishment of religion and guaranteeing religious freedom to all. In Howe's view, Stokes, while very willing to tolerate more religions than just his own Episcopalianism—indeed, more than just Christian religions—was nonetheless insensitive to the more radical thrust of those Religion Clauses. This book offers an expanded view of religious freedom.

Today, many Americans still think of religious liberty as a live-and-let-live orientation by those in the mainstream religions toward those whose religion is noticeably different. Even those who would restore teacher-led prayer in public schools would excuse any pupil who seeks exemption. Further, as many have noted, signs of a de facto established religion are still to be seen, and not just in those who would declare the United States a "Christian nation" or legislate for prayer at high school commencements and football games. For sixty years the Supreme Court's docket has seen a parade of free-exercise cases in which plaintiffs have sued for the right to do what their religion tells them to do, contrary to what the law says they should do. During the same time, the majority has repeatedly been told—with mixed signals, to be sure—that practices they thought unexceptionable were in fact offensive to others and were legally unacceptable establishments of religion. True religious liberty, in short, has been a difficult concept to comprehend and even more difficult to put into operation.

The reason for this difficulty is implied in the quotation with which this Introduction began. The inspiration underlying the Religion Clauses, though more political than religious, was a conviction that itself implied a religious stance, a religious stance moreover that many are reluctant to take or even recognize. Quoting again from Howe's review (1950:172):

> Those who support the thesis that each man should be left free by government to follow the faith which his mind and his heart prefer, very generally, if not invariably, have in religion abandoned the belief that an ultimate truth has been revealed for all and, as truth, is binding on all.

Needless to say, perhaps, but necessary to the story to be unfolded here, if Howe is correct in this assertion (and I believe he is), those who have *not* "abandoned the belief that an ultimate truth has been revealed for all" are unable to live comfortably with the American religious jurisprudence that has been unfolding during the second half of this century.

It is not that all *Americans* must relinquish their faith in the ultimacy of their religion. It is rather that the American *government*—which in governing must judge what is and is not religiously permissible—is itself required, by the twin demands of the Religion Clauses, to remain agnostic or secular. To do anything else is to favor one faith over another, or faith over nonfaith. Many Americans find this governmental secular role distasteful and claim that nonfaith is being preferred over faith. Far from "establishing" secularism, however, this stance of neutrality toward all religions is simply the design that guarantees maximum free exercise of religion for all citizens. Not surprisingly, therefore, as the implications of this stance have become clearer, so has the notion of what may be freely exercised, as well as what may not be governmentally sponsored; both First Amendment Religion Clauses now extend considerably past their late-eighteenth-century boundaries.

As for the "predominantly Protestant attitude" that lies behind the U.S. Constitution's Religion Clauses, that too is not surprising. The fundamental premise of Protestant theology is that each individual is responsible for his or her relationship to God. Not only does this premise breed suspicion of any worldly religious authority beyond the self, it also encourages a view that today's religious beliefs should be held with some tentativeness. As Pastor John Robinson said in his farewell sermon to the Mayflower Pilgrims as they prepared to leave Leyden for Massachusetts, "The Lord hath more light yet to break forth out of his Holy Word" (Hudson and Corrigan 1992:32). What Howe called "the radical principle" of religious liberty was thus inherent in the Puritanism which contributed to the thinking that led to the Constitution. (That, indeed, is the central thesis of Howe's book of 1965, *The Garden and the Wilderness*.)

So while this Protestant ancestry does not mean that today the United States has a Protestant Establishment, it *has* led to a "protestantized" American legal culture. In the oft-quoted words of G. K. Chesterton, America is "a nation with the soul of a church." Put another way, there is a discernible "religiousness" implied in the Constitution. America has many religions, all of which are supposed to experience maximum liberty, but, at the same time, American legal theory embraces an ideology that, among other things, justifies that religious liberty. Many have called this ideology a "civil" religion. The many religions are entirely voluntary and enjoy minimal governmental interference, while the "civil" religion exists more or less as an involuntary ethos, more celebrated or ignored than worshiped, more implicit than direct in its impact, more a code than a creed. Most certainly it is more the subject matter of judges than of clergy.

What follows gives these various themes expanded treatment. Chapter 1 covers the well-known ground of two competing views of church-state separation—the accommodationist view and the separationist view. The first will be equated with religious toleration, the second with the "radical principle" of religious liberty. Chapter 2 is more historical and discusses how in America the notion of religious liberty has developed in a direction of greater and greater latitude, though not, of course, without periodic reversals. While the materials of chapters 1 and 2 are familiar to many, they serve as a foundation for the remainder of the book, especially for readers with little grounding in contemporary church-state jurisprudence.

Chapter 3 argues that the logic inherent in the "radical principle" of religious liberty has led to the recognition that "conscience" is entitled to the same rights as "religion." This expansion of the notion of religious liberty to include the "rights of conscience" exposes the free-exercise part of church-state separation in its most radical form. In this exposure, the state can be said to be protecting not one or another doctrinal stance but rather any—at least, potentially any—profoundly held conviction, whether articulated in traditional religious language or otherwise. It is the *fact of conviction,* then, not the *substance* of what is held with conviction that government protects.

Religious liberty as the protection of the conscientious positions of citizens thus becomes an operable criterion for deciding what may *not* be sponsored by the state and also exposes in radical form the meaning of the Establishment Clause. This perspective is the subject of chapter 4.

The fifth chapter looks at the foundation for social order. Just as religious free exercise was never understood to be unlimited, so may conscientious claims be denied by the state. But on what basis? Just as important: On what basis may the state endorse a policy that happens to be identical to *some* persons' conscientious claims and enforce that policy on *all?*

The sixth and final chapter then discusses the inexorable political consequence of pursuing these radical principles of religious liberty in our religiously plural society. The argument is that—in expanding religious rights to include conscience—society increasingly locates the protected rights in individuals rather than in churches. That is to say, the Religion Clauses have largely become understood to say what *persons* may do out of conviction (the Free Exercise doctrine) and what religious *collectivities*—or the state on their behalf—may *not* do (the No Establishment doctrine). As a result, much of the religiousness surrounding moral matters is found in the judicial system that ensures individual religious rights. Legal institutions replace churches as the place where society (as distinct from the individual) engages the profoundest ethical issues, and legal-moral language replaces theology. The consequence may not quite deserve the label "civil religion," but it is, chapter 6 will argue, the protestantized religious faith that, Mark DeWolfe Howe suggested, lies behind the Constitution. It is a faith more in process than in substance, but a discernible substance is nonetheless there.

This volume's thesis parallels one made in my 1992 monograph, *Religion and Personal Autonomy: The Third Disestablishment in America.* There I suggested that because religion in America has become so much a matter strictly of individual choice, churches are losing their capacity to mediate communal values. If religion is decreasingly "inherited"—that is, decreasingly linked to other social structures, especially family and kinship—and churches have lost enforcement power and cannot expect government to step in and help, then a fundamental change has overtaken them. However important the church may be to individuals on a voluntary basis, its relationship to other institutions has been irretrievably altered. Among these other institutions, of course, is the state, and, because the nature of church-state relations is to be found now in judicial decision making, it is to that arena I turn here. My purpose, however, is not that of most analysts of church-state decisions: to find the line that properly separates the church from the state. If such a line exists, finding it and articulating it is a task for legal scholars. Mine is a sociological, not a legal, task. It is my aim, by looking at the circumstances surrounding church-and-state cases, to understand the broader situation where the religious and the political in America are not only *not* separate but in fact converge. I am looking for the religion *of* the Constitution by looking at the way the Constitution separates church and state. In so doing, I discern the religion *behind* the Constitution.

My purpose can be stated another way: I am not attempting to specify what church-state law *is* but where it is *heading.* Indeed, I draw—especially in chapter 4—more upon dissenting opinions as reflecting what will be, not what now prevails. It is no coincidence that the issues discussed in chapter 4 are therefore among the issues that most profoundly divide American culture.

I admit to another reason for writing this book. I am disturbed by the apparent success the Christian Right is having in disguising their effort to curtail religious liberty by declaring themselves in favor merely of "religious equality." Without an understanding of the history and subsequent development of the First Amendment, people can all too easily be persuaded by the argument that religious equality means majority rule—that, for example, if most students and their parents want prayer at their high school commencement, Free Exercise logic demands that it be allowed. As we shall be seeing, that understanding is exactly contrary to the notion that religious liberty is "inalienable," a conception that was clearly in the Framers' minds.

THE SEPARATION
OF CHURCH AND STATE:
TWO APPROACHES

Except for the very young, almost all Americans take religion seriously. For some the concern is to be able to practice religion as they wish. For others it is to make fellow believers out of heretics. For yet others it is to keep any (or all) religion from receiving government support. And for many, it seems, the aim is to restore religion to the prominent role in public life that it is thought once to have played. Obviously, religion can be taken seriously in many ways.

Those persons who conceived of the United States and designed our Constitution to be its foundational document were, on the subject of religion, of one mind about two things: They did not want the federal government to sponsor any church, and they wanted citizens to enjoy maximum free choice in how, and even whether, to practice religion. Thus, the First Amendment to the U.S. Constitution prohibits the government from making any law "respecting an establishment of religion" or interfering with the "free exercise" of religion.

For most people, in most circumstances, a literal or naive understanding of these prohibitions is adequate. To them the first prohibition means simply that the government may not put a stamp of approval on one or more religions, thereby disapproving others. The second means that persons are free to go to the church of their choice or to no church at all. Such a literal understanding, however, is inadequate for other people in other circumstances. Take, for example, the case of people who, in being drafted into the military, are taken out of their usual communities and required to live where the government assigns them. Are they entitled to the "free exercise" of their religion? What if their religion requires a priest or rabbi, the

1

Eucharist or a minyan? By providing these things with tax funds, is not the government "establishing" one or more religions?

Two Approaches Identified

The consequence of the confusion arising from this situation (and others yet to be discussed) is that, while everyone agrees with the literal wording of the Religion Clauses of the First Amendment, people disagree on what should be sacrificed first in cases where the No Establishment demand clashes with the Free Exercise demand. There are those, on the one hand, who see a strict interpretation of No Establishment as the cost of guaranteeing true Free Exercise:

> The affirmative implication of the Establishment Clause is the establishment of the civil public order. . . . All religions gain from the settlement of the war of all sects against all. . . . The price of this truce is the banishment of religion from the public square (K. Sullivan 1992:221–22).

Or:

> [R]eligious liberty can be guaranteed only in a secular state. A secular state is not hostile to religion. It can be defined as a state that is uncommitted to any religious institution (Swomley 1987:7).

On the other hand, there are those who see the secular state not as the guarantor of free exercise but as its inhibitor:

> The naked public square is the result of political doctrine and practice that would exclude religion and religiously grounded values from the conduct of public business (Neuhaus 1984:vii).

Or:

> The Religion Clause jurisprudence of the Warren and Burger era was . . . characterized by a hostility or indifference to religion. . . . Far from protecting religious freedom against the vagaries of democratic politics, the Religion Clauses during this period became an additional instrument for

promoting the politically dominant ideology of secular liberalism (McConnell 1992:134).

It is tempting to see the first of these two approaches as favoring No Establishment over Free Exercise, and to see the second approach as the reverse—favoring Free Exercise over No Establishment. While there is some merit in this view, it obscures a very important point of difference between the two approaches. The first approach—often labeled "separationist"—not only claims to adhere strictly to the No Establishment standard; it also claims to uphold the religious freedom of individuals and thus to adhere strictly to the Free Exercise standard.

The second approach, by contrast, does not claim that people's religious free exercise *in private* is being curtailed but rather that their freedom to be religious *in public,* even *at public expense,* is unconstitutionally limited by government. It is the naked *public* square that exercises them, not any naked *private* sphere. According to this second approach, government should facilitate, even encourage, religion by making religious actions easier to perform. This approach is therefore often called "accommodationist."

Underlying the accommodationist approach is the assumption that what is to be accommodated is easy to identify. It comes in many guises, and all—within reason—are to be tolerated; no accommodationist favors one established *church*. Rather, accommodationists believe all religions are to be shown preference over nonreligion, or else religion cannot be freely exercised. For this reason, the accommodationist approach is sometimes referred to as "nonpreferentialism." By contrast, the separationist approach is based on the "radical principle" that truly guaranteeing free exercise requires government to offer no aid, give no privilege, to *any* religion, nor to religion over nonreligion. For separationists, religion is not all that easily identified.

Both viewpoints are called approaches here because neither is clear enough or coherent enough to be called a doctrine. On many issues, representatives of the two viewpoints can and do join forces. Within each viewpoint can be found differences in what deserves greatest emphasis or what should most readily be sacrificed. Despite this lack of sharp lines, however, a thrust or impulse can be located in each approach.

Take, for example, the work of Leo Pfeffer. In his book *Religion, State, and the Burger Court,* Pfeffer notes wryly that "in the field of free exercise of religion and church-state separation . . . I consistently defend a position called absolutist or extremist or doctrinaire or unrealistic or uncompromising" (1984:xi). What that implies is that for him the No Establishment Clause means no accommodation of religion whatsoever. I heard Pfeffer at a 1981 conference declare that in his view a Roman Catholic hospital should receive no public funding if it so much as has a statue of the Virgin Mary somewhere on its premises. Pfeffer's point, of course, did not indicate hostility to Catholicism per se, for he would feel similarly about a Protestant, Jewish, or Muslim hospital that displayed symbols of its faith. What it indicated was his conviction that in exchange for the right to be Catholic, and to operate a Catholic facility—however slight the Catholicity might be—Catholics and their church must give up government aid of any kind. Correlatively, a hospital, to receive such aid, must relinquish all signs of religion. As we shall be observing later, such an extreme position is easily challenged. Would Pfeffer deny the Catholic hospital fire protection, for example? How about tax exemption as a charitable organization? It is enough for now to say simply that the "separationists" can be seen to stretch along a continuum, with Pfeffer perhaps at the extreme and others at various points closer to the stance called accommodationist.

Likewise with the accommodationists. James K. Fitzpatrick can represent their approach as the counterpart to Leo Pfeffer. In *God, Country, and the Supreme Court,* Fitzpatrick writes: "The basic standards of vice and virtue embodied in the laws of Europe and America . . . are expressions of the consciences of the people of the West, consciences formed by their immersion in the Christian Faith" (1985:198–99). In Fitzpatrick's view the people who wrote and ratified the U.S. Constitution never intended their society to depart from "a Christian way of life" (viii). Because he sees America as "increasingly de-Christianized," he recommends reconsideration of "the wisdom of the God-centered political order of Europe's Old Regime" (x), in other words, an Established Church.

Fitzpatrick, like Pfeffer, can also be easily challenged, especially if his position is understood literally to advocate an establishment of religion. Seen, however, as a call for governmental assistance in the moral renewal of America, as a call for governmental sponsorship of virtue, its appeal is readily comprehended. Both approaches have their attractions.

Two Approaches Distinguished

If neither approach can be etched sharply enough to be called a doctrine, still it is possible to distinguish separationists from accommodationists on a number of related issues. Take, for example, the matter of "original intent," the question of what the authors of the Constitution meant by their choice of words. Understandably, neither judges nor the public knowingly adopt positions they believe to be contrary to what the Founders intended. On the other hand, considerable disagreement exists over such questions as:

1. Can we know the *real* intentions of persons writing over 200 years ago?
2. Should we be faithful to the *words* they employed or to what we think they meant to *convey* by those words?
3. Since so much in modern life was simply unknown to the Constitution's writers, we must extrapolate from the "spirit" of what they wrote, but how are we to understand what that spirit *is?*

Thus American legal culture renders the U.S. Constitution much the way Christian culture renders the Bible or Muslim culture the Koran. As Sanford Levinson has pointed out (1988:18ff.), just as there are "literalists" and "modernists" when it comes to interpreting the Bible, and just as there are some who look upon the Bible as the sole authority and others who regard tradition and/or later revelation as additional authoritative sources, so are there comparable divisions when it comes to interpreting the Constitution.

In a very general sense, then, accommodationists are inclined toward the view that (a) the original intent of the Constitution writers can be known,

(b) their words should be understood literally, and (c) extrapolating from those words should be rare and should be done only with great care. Separationists, by contrast, are more inclined to see the need to *interpret* the Constitution because (a) "original intent" can never be known with certainty, (b) words written two centuries ago may have undergone changes in meaning, and (c) extrapolating from those words, though of course to be done with great care, is required and required frequently.

The source of these differences is easy to see in the contrasting views the two approaches have of modernity. Both approaches of course recognize that modern America is vastly different from late-eighteenth-century America—vastly more pluralistic religiously, vastly more commercial and urban, and vastly more bureaucratized. Where they differ is in their notions of what the judicial role, and hence the Constitution's role, is in adjusting to these changes. Separationists are likely to give a big role to the judiciary; accommodationists are likely to prefer that the legislative branch, not the courts, make the adjustments.

Ronald Dworkin (1993:26) says that the fundamental issue comes down to

> whether the Constitution should be understood as a limited list of the particular individual rights that statesmen now dead thought important, or as a commitment to abstract ideals of political morality that each generation of citizens, lawyers, and judges must together explore and reinterpret. I shall argue that the first answer is indefensible, in spite of its apparent popularity among conservative members of the present Supreme Court.

Dworkin is a separationist, and those he calls "conservative members of the present Supreme Court" are accommodationists. We shall encounter these persons in later chapters.

A component of the issue of original intent is the question of just how the Constitution writers expressed their concern for religion: Separationists believe they desired to keep government away from religion, thus "protecting" individual believers; accommodationists perceive those writers' preference for religious organizations. We saw that James K. Fitzpatrick imagined the Founders to be Christian, at least in spirit if not in church membership. Evidence does not support that extreme position. For instance, Fitzpatrick states, "Well over 90 percent of eighteenth-century Americans were members of church congregations" (1985:viii), thereby hoping to buttress his claim of a "Christian"-based Constitution. The latest and most carefully drawn estimate of church adherents in 1776, however, is 17 percent (Finke and Stark 1992:27). That the Founders were sensitive to religion there can be no doubt, but, as Mark DeWolfe Howe forcefully argues, they were chiefly concerned that "intruders from the federal wilderness would not trespass in the gardens of religion" (1965:172). Certainly they knew Christianity best, but they knew about other religions as well and sought freedom for all, including nontheists. They were protecting, in Jefferson's well-known phrase, "the Jew and Gentile, the Christian and Mahometan, the Hindoo, and infidel of every denomination" (quoted in Davis 1993:92).

Given widespread acceptance in today's America of religious liberty and religious pluralism, the debate over how "Christian" this nation *was* at its birth pales in significance when compared with a parallel question just now implied: Was nonreligion or irreligion to be given the same rights as religion? As Phillip E. Johnson puts it (1984:818):

> Practically everyone agrees that government ought not to take sides between Catholic, Protestant, and Jew. It is not equally clear, however, that government can or should be neutral as between atheism and theism, nor is it clear whether neutrality implies strictly excluding sectarian symbols from public ceremonies or displays.

Here again the separationists and accommodationists differ. Leonard Levy makes a strong argument that the Framers could *not* have favored religion over irreligion (1986:86), while Howe makes an equally strong argument that they did indeed favor religion over irreligion (1965:161).

Keep in mind that many of the original thirteen states allowed towns to give tax support to churches (chiefly for the education of children), and they continued to do so well past the adoption of the Constitution. Nobody claims that religion was not favored at the state level. So the debate about federal favoritism might be moot, were it not for the Fourteenth Amendment, following the Civil War, which, through its Due Process Clause, eventually incorporated federally protected rights into the laws of every state. (The Free Exercise Clause was incorporated in 1940 in the *Cantwell* case, the Establishment Clause in 1947 in the *Everson* case. See the Appendix, page 113, for complete citations for these and all other cases discussed in this book.)

The question thus becomes whether such incorporation today makes unconstitutional a religious establishment at the state level. In other words, may a state, if not the federal government, favor religion over irreligion? Accommodationists—at least some of them—would say yes, because indeed the Framers favored religion, acknowledging only that a *national* establishment was not permitted. Separationists—at least some of them—would say no, because the Framers meant to protect the freedom not to be religious at all.

This difference might seem exotic now, given the unlikelihood of an established church anywhere in the United States today. But the issue underlying this difference—the issue that distinguishes the separationist from the accommodationist—is very real: Does the First Amendment say that religious differences are merely to be tolerated, or is the right to be religiously different inalienable? And, if the latter, does that right include the right not to be religious at all?

As with the constitutional prohibition against a federally established religion, but given the fact of state-established churches well into the nineteenth century, room remains for earnest debate on this right to be nonreligious. Take, for example, the case of Pennsylvania, often held up as an early paragon of religious liberty. Its first constitution declared the inalienable right of conscience. Nonetheless, officeholders in that state had to confess a belief in God and in the divine inspiration of the Old and New Testaments. Religious discrimination, in other words, was common—against Catholics, Jews, some Protestants, and certainly the irreligious.

Does it matter, then, whether the writers of the Constitution "intended" to favor religion over irreligion or "intended" to grant religious liberty to the nonreligious? Does it matter whether the words they used are literally understood?

Of course it matters from the standpoint of historical accuracy, though we will never know what those writers of the Constitution "really" intended. For purposes of present-day decision making, however, whether the Framers favored religion over irreligion hardly matters for separationists but matters greatly for accommodationists. The complicated reasons for this difference will be taken up later, but suffice it here to say that, from the separationist perspective, the Constitution was written at a time when the word "religion" had a common meaning, and now it does not. In other words, separationists want government to favor and protect everything they think it is that the Framers *then* had in mind by religion, including conscience. But they find in today's world that the word "religion" no longer adequately covers all such phenomena. Instead, in the effort to protect the consciences of all individuals, government refrains (with qualifications yet to be discussed) from endorsing anybody's conscience. This has the effect of allowing free play of everybody's conscientious efforts, whether "religious" or not, without regarding some of those efforts as privileged *because* they are religious.

Accommodationists, on the other hand, do not agree that individual religious liberty is best protected when the government is religiously neutral, when, in the already quoted words of Kathleen Sullivan (1992:222), religion is "banished" from the public square. Accommodationists want religion to have a privileged place, in public as well as in private matters. They do distinguish between religion and conscience. They believe, as Stephen Carter puts it (1993:134), that neutrality

> treats religious belief as a matter of individual choice, an aspect of conscience, with which the government must not interfere but which it has no obligation to respect. . . . Accommodation, however, can be crafted into a tool that accepts religion as a group rather than an individual activity. When accommodation is so understood, corporate worship, not individual conscience, becomes the obstacle around which state policy must make the widest possible berth. . . . Thus, the reason for accommodation becomes not the protection of individual conscience, but the preservation of the religions as independent power bases that exist in large part in order to resist the state.

What accommodationists therefore seek—government help in preserving "religions" and "corporate worship"—separationists view as the improper desire for establishment status. They fear that those religions with the greatest number of adherents would benefit most from "state policy," while minority religions, and of course the nonreligious, would be discriminated against or ignored. For separationists, this is an insidious effort to achieve precisely what the No Establishment Clause prohibits. As Sullivan says, "Majority practices are myopically seen by their own practitioners as uncontroversial" (1992:207). Richard Jones (1986) provides an excellent analysis of these two approaches.

Public and Private Religion

Throughout the discussion thus far I have made repeated reference to religion in public and religion in private. It is clear that the accommodationist approach would allow, even encourage, a larger public role for religion, and the separationist approach would not. Since both approaches of course agree that—privately—Americans may be religious in virtually any way they desire, it is tempting to cast the difference between the approaches as a matter of whether religion is to be *only* private or is to be extended also into the public sphere. But this phrasing is not quite correct. Separationists have, in principle, no objection to religion's *presence* in public; what they object to is religion's public presence in a manner that has or implies government *endorsement*. And what accommodationists object to is that, in avoiding any act that might appear to be an endorsement, government is emptying the public sphere of all religious influence. This situation, they contend, contradicts American constitutional history.

Harold J. Berman (1989:71–72) puts the matter succinctly:

What distinguishes most sharply our situation in the latter half of the twentieth century from that of the previous centuries is the fact that in our public discourse separation of church and state has come to mean separation of religion and government, and this in turn has stripped much of our political discourse of its religious dimension.

This controversy over religion's proper role in public is manifested in at least two ways. First is the obvious issue of endorsement per se. Take, for example, the treatment of religion in the public schools. Accommodationists are often portrayed as wanting to coerce students, via the apparatus of teachers, curriculum, assemblies, and so on, to pray and read the Bible. Separationists, in contrast, are portrayed as wanting to keep everything religious out of public schools. These portraits can be exaggerated, because neither approach necessarily stands in the way of teaching *about* religion. However, when some accommodationists complain that merely teaching about religion fails to communicate religion adequately (that "You need to be a believer yourself to teach it"), they are revealed to be wanting what the No Establishment Clause prohibits: the state's *approval* of religion. Similarly, when some separationists complain that religion cannot be taught in a neutral fashion and therefore should be outlawed, they are revealed to be wanting what the same clause prohibits: the state's *disapproval* of religion.

The second way by which the controversy over religion's public role is manifested is more subtle, having to do with how and when individuals may invoke their religion in public discussion. Accommodationists want special warrant given to religious claims; separationists would allow such claims to be heard but deny them special warrant. Consider Stephen Carter's complaint (1993:23):

> One good way to end a conversation . . . is to tell a group of well-educated professionals that you hold a political position . . . because it is required by your understanding of God's will. In the unlikely event that anyone hangs around to talk to you about it, the chances are that you will be challenged on the ground that you are intent on imposing your religious beliefs on other people.

Does it not seem more likely that those listeners would expect to hear a justification for the political position in terms they can be expected to recognize, whether or not they shared the speaker's particular understanding of God's will? The religious freedom people have—to arrive at different understandings of God's will—is precisely the situation that, in *public* discussion, denies special warrant to anybody's claim in the name of religion. Even Richard John Neuhaus, whose book *The Naked Public Square* makes clear that he shares much of Carter's viewpoint, states: "Those who want to bring religiously based values to bear in public discourse have an obligation to 'translate' those values into terms that are as accessible as possible to those who do not share the same religious grounding" (1984:125).

That Carter seems not to comprehend this admonition is puzzling to separationists. They wonder why Carter, for example, speaking no doubt for other accommodationists, claims that his book *The Culture of Disbelief* tries "to discover whether there might be a way to preserve the separation of church and state without trivializing faith as we do today" (1993:15). Separationists respond that, far from trivializing faith, the fact that no religion may legitimately claim the state's support, and nobody's faith can be imposed on another, is what allows all faiths to be freely exercised. To expect religious motivation to be sufficient justification in a discussion with others not sharing that motivation is to invite precisely the religious wars the First Amendment seeks to avoid.

Accommodationists, of course, are not without response. Steven Smith, for example, asserts baldly that the "ideal of religious neutrality is simply not coherent" (1995:94). He goes on to explain why:

> The problem, simply put, is that theories of religious freedom seek to reconcile or to mediate among competing religious and secular positions within a society, but those positions disagree about the very background beliefs on which a theory of religious freedom must rest. . . . In adopting a theory of religious freedom that is consistent with some background beliefs and not with others, therefore, government must adopt, or privilege, one of the competing secular or religious positions. Yet this adopting or preferring . . . is precisely what modern theories of religious freedom seek to avoid (1995:68).

With one major qualification (to be discussed in chapter 6), separationists are in no position to disagree with this explanation. Their claim simply is that only by adopting a secular position can a society guarantee religious liberty, while accommodationists claim that by thus "establishing" secularism, the state thereby inhibits religious practice in the public square. Separationists agree, but, quoting Sullivan again, that is "the price of this truce" (1992:222). The qualification, as we shall see in chapter 6, is that "established secularism" is something of a misnomer, since underlying that position is a discernible religious perspective. It is the attitude that Mark DeWolfe Howe, as we saw in the Introduction, called "predominantly Protestant in spirit." In chapter 6 I call it the religion "behind" the Constitution.

From Accommodation
to Separation

Perhaps by now the reader will have surmised that I have greater sympathy for the separationist than for the accommodationist position. A major reason is found in my training as a sociologist, a point that, when elaborated, reveals yet another difference between the two approaches. Thus, accommodationists tend to believe that the status of church-state separation is simply a matter of political choice. Neuhaus, for example, says that privatized religion is a "widely accepted idea" and that church-state separation is a "supported axiom" (1984:20). Both statements may be true, but, even if true, that does not mean religion is privatized and church and state are separate *because* they are "accepted" and "supported." It can be argued that both phenomena are the inevitable consequences of social forces that operate whether or not people desire or accept them. More specifically, were people to withdraw their consent to living with these consequences, other consequences even more objectionable would ensue—at least that is the theory behind the Religion Clauses.

Now of course any ordered society depends upon the consent of the governed; withdrawal of that consent will tend to produce chaos and anarchy. But chaos and anarchy are not the means by which just any preferred state of affairs can be created. Take as an illustration, once again, the matter of state-sponsored prayer in public schools, no doubt a near-universal practice at one time in this nation's history (and still practiced far more than the public realizes, though clearly outlawed since the early 1960s). Decline in this practice did not result simply from a change of mind by citizens. Rather, school boards, principals, teachers, and parents—and eventually lawmakers in various states—were faced with dilemmas such as which sacred scripture to read or which rendition of the Lord's Prayer to recite. In other words, they came to feel pressure to honor everyone's religious sensibilities. These dilemmas were in turn brought about by increased religious pluralism but also by a population that was heterogenizing in many ways. Moreover, school attendance was mandated for all children, and Protestantism was no longer the assumed "choice" of all constituents of the public schools. Some flexibility existed in just how decision makers responded to these dilemmas, but simply polling people's preferences was not among the choices. (However, school prayers continue in some districts because they are perceived by administrators and teachers to be the public's preference; see Dolbeare and Hammond 1971.) In other words, prohibiting schools from sponsoring religious activity was imposed by circumstances beyond anybody's control; here, as in so many other ways, religion in "public" was sacrificed in order that religion in "private" could be freely exercised.

There is a sense, then, that in two centuries of living under the Religion Clauses, American society has moved *from* a more accommodationist position *to* a more separationist position, and it has done so not simply by choice or by a change of population opinion but out of necessity. In sociological terms, this has been a "structural" shift, comparable, let us say, to the replacement of horse-drawn and railroad transportation by the automobile and airplane. While these transitions were carried out by individuals, they were not the results of particular individual choice. In the arena of church-state relations, accommodationists often overlook the structural character of this long-term shift toward greater separation; separationists are more likely to view the shift as inevitable. Chapter 2 will elaborate on these historical trends.

The Two Clauses

This long-term shift toward greater separation, while obviously evaluated differently by the two approaches, resulted in a fairly high level of consensus about how the Religion Clauses should operate in practice. Such consensus did not guarantee agreement by both camps with every decision rendered, of course, but it generally meant agreement about *how* the decision should be reached.

Regarding the Free Exercise Clause, most jurists and scholars regard as nearly absolute ("inalienable") the freedom to be religious (or not) in any way a person wishes to be. Most certainly this means that majorities may not trample on minorities' religious liberty. Widely recognized, however, is the fact that while religious freedom to *believe* as one wishes can be absolute, religious freedom to *act* on those beliefs cannot be. In drawing the line between permissible and impermissible actions, therefore, widespread consensus gives the benefit of the doubt to religiously motivated behavior *unless the state has a compelling interest* in curbing that behavior. The burden, in other words, is on the state to show *why* the behavior should be curtailed. Thus, to take an illuminating example, adults may refuse medical treatment for themselves out of religious conviction, but they may not deny their minor children such treatment. The state, it is reasoned, has a compelling interest in protecting the welfare of citizens too young to look out for themselves, but it has no such compelling interest in the case of adults.

In 1990, *Oregon Employment Division v. Smith* involved two Native Americans who confessed to using peyote in religious worship. The two were fired from their jobs and denied unemployment benefits. Justice Scalia wrote for the majority that it was enough for the Court to note that Oregon had not targeted Native Americans in putting peyote on its list of prohibited drugs, and therefore the state need not identify a compelling interest in upholding the penalty defendants received. A majority on the Court agreed. Although Justice O'Connor concurred in the majority decision, she was bothered, she wrote in her concurring opinion, by such an abandonment of "well-settled First Amendment jurisprudence."

In addition to the minority on the Court, many other Americans were bothered by this abandonment, and a groundswell of opinion and organizational collaboration arose to petition Congress. By 1993 Congress had passed the Religious Freedom Restoration Act (RFRA), which declared that the compelling interest test must be applied "in all cases where free exercise of religion is substantially burdened." One might have surmised, therefore, that the compelling interest doctrine was once again "well-settled, First Amendment jurisprudence." That proved not to be the case, however, as the Supreme Court, in June 1997, declared RFRA unconstitutional. Justice Kennedy, writing for the majority in *City of Boerne v. Flores,* said, "Broad as the power of Congress is . . . RFRA contradicts vital principles necessary to maintain separation of powers and the federal balance." Congress, in other words, had intruded into the Court's domain.

In dissent, Justice O'Connor wrote:

> I remain of the view that *Smith* was wrongly decided, and I would use this case to reexamine the Court's holding there. . . . If the Court were to correct the misinterpretation of the Free Exercise Clause set forth in *Smith,* it would simultaneously put our First Amendment jurisprudence back on course and allay the legitimate concerns of a majority in Congress. . . . We would then be in a position to review RFRA in light of a proper interpretation of the Free Exercise Clause.

As for now, the "proper" interpretation of the Free Exercise Clause is not at all clear. We shall return to the *Smith* case and *Boerne v. Flores* in chapter 3.

With regard to the No Establishment Clause, it is more accurate to say that a doctrine *was* well settled but confusion now surrounds it. This doctrine was called the "Lemon Test" because it was formalized in a 1971 Supreme Court case, *Lemon v. Kurtzman,* that ruled unconstitutional certain tax-supported programs aiding nonpublic schools. The Lemon Test requires that a publicly funded program, to be constitutional, must meet three criteria: (1) its purpose must not be either to advance or to inhibit religion, (2) its primary effect must not be either to advance or to inhibit religion, and (3) it must be free of "entangling alliances" between religion and government.

The Lemon Test appeared for a period of years to offer a way for courts to determine the constitutionality of a number of legislative actions designed especially to ease the financial burden of nonpublic schools, this in recognition that such schools relieve enrollment pressure on tax-supported public schools. Indeed, a great many cases were decided with the help of the Lemon Test, but instead of clarity and predictability these cases collectively yielded results that defied order, to the point where some accommodationists, led by Justice Rehnquist, would junk the Lemon Test altogether. Their sentiment is nicely conveyed in Rehnquist's testy dissent in *Wallace v. Jaffree* (1985), where he expressed his dismay at what the Lemon Test had wrought:

[A] State may lend to parochial school children geography textbooks that contain maps of the United States, but the State may not lend maps of the United States for use in geography class. A State may lend textbooks on American colonial history, but it may not lend a film on George Washington, or a film projector to show it in history class. A State may lend classroom workbooks but may not lend workbooks in which the parochial school children write, thus rendering them nonreusable. A State may pay for bus transportation to religious schools but may not pay for bus transportation from the parochial school, to the public zoo or natural history museum for a field trip. A State may pay for diagnostic services conducted in the parochial school, but therapeutic services must be given in a different building; speech and hearing "services" conducted by the State inside the sectarian school are forbidden, but the State may conduct speech and hearing diagnostic testing inside the sectarian school. Exceptional parochial school students may receive counseling, but it must take place outside of the parochial school, such as in a trailer parked down the street. A State may give cash to a parochial school to pay for the administration of State-written tests and State-ordered reporting services, but it may not provide funds for teacher-prepared tests on secular subjects. Religious instruction may not be given in public school, but the public school may release students during the day for religion classes elsewhere and may enforce attendance at those classes with its truancy laws.

On Muddling Through

Of course, separationists are as puzzled as accommodationists in trying to discern what, in principle, is and is not permissible. Abstract legal concepts (such as "compelling interest") that point to unambiguous decisions do not exist in the No Establishment arena as they do in the Free Exercise arena. This situation does not necessarily disturb everyone, however, in part because some kind of trade-off or compromise is widely perceived as inevitable in church-state cases; decisions that restrict the free exercise of religion can be understood to be giving preference to ("establishing") religions not requiring such restriction, just as decisions that prohibit programs on No Establishment grounds can be understood as narrowing somebody's free exercise. But apparently many Americans live comfortably with the resulting "muddle." As law professor Phillip E. Johnson says, "If we judge our constitutional law regarding religion on the basis of its acceptability to persons of widely differing religious opinions rather than its conceptual coherency, it looks a great deal better" (1984:840).

Even if society can muddle through establishment cases, however, pressures exist to seek and declare the principles by which people in general, and jurists in particular, can know what is and is not permissible. And, of course, since separationists and accommodationists respond differently to these pressures, legal clarity in establishment cases may be a long time coming. On the other hand, a kind of sociological clarity regarding "establishment" may be closer at hand, and that will be the focus of chapter 4.

The Rise of
Church-State Issues

There remains now the task of asking why church-state issues have become so vexatious in recent decades. Several answers can be suggested, but first the question must be sharpened. Until passage of the Fourteenth Amendment after the Civil War, an amendment that step by step guaranteed "due process" to all U.S. citizens and thus "incorporated" the federal constitutional rights into the various state constitutions, First Amendment issues arose only in the territories, not states, of the Union. They were, therefore, few in number. (One of these, *Reynolds v. United States* [1879], is exceedingly important to the argument of this book because, in ruling Mormon polygamy unconstitutional, the Court enunciated the distinction between the absolute freedom of belief and the not-so-absolute freedom of behavior.) Moreover, as already noted, "incorporation" of the Religion Clauses did not occur until 1940 in *Cantwell v. Connecticut,* another case of enormous importance to our story line, as will be seen in chapter 3. (Technically, *Cantwell* incorporated Free Exercise; Establishment was incorporated in *Everson,* 1947.)

As it happens, therefore, Religion Clause jurisprudence—especially the kind of jurisprudence that applies to modern-day church-state conflicts—dates back little more than a half century. It is not surprising, then, that so many issues have arisen in recent decades. Over and beyond this collapsed history of church-state jurisprudence, however, at least four reasons can be offered for the central place religion has had in the legal controversies of the second half of the twentieth century.

The first of these, to be developed more fully in chapter 2, is simply that the United States began as a de facto Protestant society and was widely seen as such until late in the nineteenth century, and it has taken much of the twentieth century to awaken to the constitutional implications for religious life in our times (see Handy 1991; Hammond 1992).

The second reason is coincident with this spread of religious pluralism and decline of Protestant hegemony. It is the massive increase in governmental intervention in the lives of Americans, including their religious lives. From building codes to government grants to social agencies to civil rights commissions and regulations of the airwaves, government at all levels simply has far more occasions to intersect religion. The ideal of the "separation" of church and state, if it were ever a realistic possibility, is certainly not possible now.

A third reason for the increased appearance of church-state issues is the elaboration, and especially the increased visibility, of religions in the United States that, by not conforming more or less to Judeo-Christian traditions, often challenge accepted procedures, many of which end up in courts of law. A vivid example is the 1993 case *Church of the Lukumi Babalu Aye, Inc. v. City of Hialeah.* This religion, called Santeria, made up of African religious beliefs and practices brought into this hemisphere with slavery, mixed with Roman Catholicism and accretions over time from the Caribbean, has emerged in the United States in recent years among immigrants from that region. It has also made converts here. The church in this case found facilities in Hialeah, Florida, for carrying out its central rituals, including the sacrificing by knife of chickens, goats, and other animals, which were then cooked and eaten. The City Council of Hialeah passed legislation prohibiting such actions within the city limits, but the U.S. Supreme Court unanimously ruled that the legislation was clearly aimed at inhibiting the free exercise of religion, and Hialeah had no compelling interest for enacting such an inhibition.

The Hialeah case is merely a recent example of a minority religion, however. Many of the early cases of the modern period involved Jehovah's Witnesses, although so-called "new religious movements," especially Scientology, have in recent years replaced them as the chief litigators in novel challenges on both Free Exercise and No Establishment grounds (Robbins 1993; Richardson 1995). Most of these recent cases have been heard in lower courts, however, very few having reached the Supreme Court.

The popularity of these new religious movements, if not their origins, lay in the cultural shock that began in the 1960s in America, a shock not yet over. It is this cultural shock that provides the fourth reason for many of the church-state cases on today's dockets. Following the model offered by William G. McLoughlin (who, in turn, was following the model of Anthony F. C. Wallace [1956]), one can note that the 1960s set in motion a number of profound challenges to the status quo. McLoughlin was overly optimistic in asserting it would only take thirty years—one generation—to absorb those challenges, respond with more adaptable normative guidelines, and reach a stage where parents would once again raise children in more or less the same fashion that they themselves had been raised (1978:chap. 1). Perhaps the challenges have been too vast, cover too many social activities, and may even be too contradictory to bring a new stability in a single generation. The challenges, after all, involved the environment, foreign war, ethnic conflict, drugs, the work ethic, and—above all—family and sexual values. Perhaps it is no wonder that the American nation still reels from the shock.

McLoughlin, however, made the strategic point that, as a result of the challenge to the status quo of the 1960s, one could expect a "revitalization" movement to emerge, a movement that not only would reject the alternatives being offered in preference to the status quo but would also reassert the virtue of the "good old days" preceding that status quo, a movement that would, so to speak, favor turning back the clock. Imagining itself to be a "reform" effort, its real desire would be to "re-form" a society idealistically remembered.

Efforts, then, were made to reassert the authority of parents over children and husbands over wives, to reject divorce, premarital and homosexual sex, and of course abortion. Accompanying these efforts are certain strategies for bringing them about, such as returning to sponsored prayer in public schools, tax vouchers for use in sectarian schools, legislative acts that would restrict abortion or deny welfare payment to unwed mothers. It is, then, many of these latter strategies that have made their way into court, often emerging as church-state cases, thus increasing both the number and the vexatiousness of First Amendment issues. We shall encounter several such cases in chapter 4.

The political scientist Matthew C. Moen offers a splendid confirming analysis in his *Transformation of the Christian Right* (1992). Especially in his chapter 6 does he show how fundamentalist and other evangelical Christians came to recognize the futility of arguing for the "old morality" on the grounds of moral superiority alone and now argue their case on the grounds of civil liberties. Thus they claim that schoolchildren are being denied "free exercise" when they cannot pray in school, and abortion protesters are denied "free speech" when bubble laws keep them a certain distance from clinic personnel and their patients.

Conclusion

No doubt there are yet other reasons why church-state cases are so often in the news and in the courts. Courts are mechanisms for resolving particular conflicts, but there is no reason to believe religious conflict will once and for all be settled, any more than there is reason to imagine a world with no conflict at all. The *character* of religious conflict changes, however, and the remaining chapters of this book are an effort to understand something of that change as it has unfolded in this century.

2

FROM ACCOMMODATION TO SEPARATION

Toward the end of the last chapter I asserted that, since the founding of the United States, American society has shifted toward greater and greater government neutrality toward religion. I made no effort to document the assertion at the time but used it to show in yet another way how the two approaches to church-state relations differ. Separationists perceive the structural inevitability, given the premises of the Constitution and Bill of Rights, of the shift toward greater neutrality and thus both accept and applaud it. Accommodationists, by contrast, not only dislike greater neutrality but do not regard it as inevitable; indeed, they often suggest that stanching, even reversing, that shift needs only the willpower of those in authority. It is time now to document the shift and thus settle the issue. Fortunately, the shift is widely acknowledged, so citing some of the major literature on the subject can make this section brief.

Some International Comparisons

Let us begin by looking at the international context for church-state relations, where we will see that many of the same structural forces making for government neutrality toward religion found in America are found also in other nation-states.

Many Americans take justifiable pride in the religious liberty guaranteed by the U.S. Constitution. As we saw in chapter 1, judging by the *relative* lack of religious conflict in U.S. history, one might surmise that American citizens are reasonably content with the "muddle through" process by which church-state decisions are reached by courts of law, and that is probably true.

It would be a mistake, however, to imagine that America's constitutional solution to church-and-state matters was simply invented out of the blue by a handful of theorists whose thinking was unencumbered by processes they experienced and observed. Minimally, at least two kinds of processes converged late in the eighteenth century among the Framers that led them to the Religion Clauses. One was the fervor of Puritan Protestantism; the other was Enlightenment liberalism. The first wanted assurance that government would not meddle in church affairs; the second, assurance that the church would not meddle in government affairs. Put in other words, the Framers were mindful of the religious pluralism in their midst and the mischief that can result when religion and politics confront each other.

These circumstances, however, were not unique to the newly founded United States. Whether the American doctrine of religious liberty was "derivative" from the British as E. R. Norman claims (1968:4) may be debatable, but what is beyond debate is the fact that many nations were facing up to the church-state implications of (1) increased religious pluralism and (2) emerging state involvement in activities traditionally carried out in the private sector. England and the United States may have responded to these implications earlier and more explicitly, but responses have been required of all nations. This fact is important to our argument, because the demand for a response, once met, does not disappear but reappears in ever-changing ways. Without this understanding, the shift from accommodation to separation in American church-state relations is easily misinterpreted.

Research by N. J. Demerath III is of considerable help at this point. In the summer 1991 issue of *Daedalus,* Demerath published some research findings on church-state relations in four nations, all with at least nominally established religions: Indonesia, Pakistan, Sweden, and Thailand. As he says (1991:38), his findings are "surprising":

Despite religion's prominence as a source of political legitimacy and campaign rhetoric [in all four places], it is rarely a dominant factor in the affairs of state. The United States is less distinctive in this regard than many Americans suppose, and insofar as its own tradition of "church-state separation" continues, this may owe less to legal and constitutional requirements than to a range of social and political constraints which we share with other nations.

Demerath offers several reasons why he found more neutrality (that is, more separation of church and state) in these nominally non-neutral nations than might have been expected. First, despite having "official" religions, all four nations are in fact religiously plural, with Pakistan for example having both Sunni and Shiite Muslims, a situation making suspect any real power exercised by Islamic courts or mullahs. Second, religion is more likely invoked at election time but then later regarded by officials as a liability in the compromise realm of actual governance. A third reason why religion carries less clout in these nominally religious states is their increasing involvement in the international political economy. In both politics and the economy, the major decision making is more and more being carried out by bureaucratized civil servants, persons beholden to forces, including foreign obligations, existing quite independent of current elected politicians.

No gauge exists to measure just how neutral toward religion these nations are, relative to the United States and each other, but no need exists here for such a device. It is enough to note two things: (1) in all four instances, the "religiousness" of the state has declined while the degree of "separation" has increased, and (2) the reasons for these changes are structural—results that nobody wills into existence but instead are inevitable outcomes of the active pursuit of other goals. The situation in the United States is comparable, as will now be explored in some detail.

What Happened

To argue that "established" religion and thus accommodation has declined in America, while government neutrality and thus separation has increased, is *not* to claim that American government is now absolutely neutral. As Milton Himmelfarb says, "In every Western nation, Christianity is too inseparable from the national culture for religious neutrality to be truly possible" (1968:286). But Himmelfarb's statement should be understood to mean that the American culture retains some vestiges of Christianity (as it certainly does), not that it remains "as Christian" as it once was. One must readily grant that the roots of American culture included Christianity, and for nearly a century the U.S. Constitution was interpreted in light of those roots. But events occurred that altered that interpretation and caused governments at all levels to become more neutral toward all religions, including Christianity.

Consider these illustrations:

1. Until well into the nineteenth century, the Protestant Bible was a major textbook in schools, seen less as a sectarian instrument than an element of common culture.

2. "Religion," of the sort mentioned in the First Amendment, was, during the same time, largely understood to mean worship, so that "free exercise" was thought to refer to freedom to worship how one liked, and "no establishment" meant that government did not impose worship on anybody.

3. Tax money given to a church and its minister to conduct school was not seen as an "establishment" of religion because, until the 1830s, no other kind of school was known, and schools were thought necessary for the moral education of citizens.

To be sure, there were some people such as Jefferson and Madison who hoped that the U.S. Constitution would be understood in the more separationist manner that is employed today. That hope was not widespread, however, and—while religion was, for the most part, freely exercised—vestiges of "establishment" abounded and did so with legal blessing.

For example, the dominant jurist of the first half of the nineteenth century, Joseph Story, saw no inconsistency in advocating Christianity as the model to be used by the government in the promotion of morality. A

Supreme Court Justice from 1811 to 1845, Story is credited with influencing the ways that individual states adjudicated church-state matters, partly through his three-volume *Commentaries on the Constitution of the United States*. Story wrote (1833:726, 728):

> Probably at the time of the adoption of the constitution . . . the general, if not the universal, sentiment in America was that Christianity ought to receive encouragement from the state, so far as was not incompatible with the private rights of conscience and the freedom of religious worship. . . . [The] real object of the [First] amendment was not to countenance, much less to advance Mahometanism, or Judaism, or infidelity, by prostrating Christianity; but to exclude all rivalry among Christian sects, and to prevent any national ecclesiastical establishment.

We will see presently that Story's understanding of the No Establishment Clause—that it was meant to exclude "all rivalry among Christian sects"—was still in force on the Georgia Supreme Court as late as 1922. (In fairness to Story, however, note should be made that he began his statement with the word "Probably." Other evidence from Story's writing makes clear that, as a Calvinist-turned-Unitarian, he was committed both to religious liberty and to the notion that public virtue was exemplified in "Christianity." The difficulty in holding these two views in tension is, of course, exactly what has generated the separationist process.)

These practices were challenged in due time. Roman Catholics insisted on the use of the Douay Bible in public schools and, when turned down, built a network of parochial schools. The issue of tax support for schooling thus became problematic. Freedom to worship as one liked presented little difficulty until, for example, the claim to polygamy redefined what it was that could be freely exercised. Finally, a public school system, with professionally trained teachers, emerged to replace church-operated schools.

A main point, of course, is that no one wished these changes into existence; they came with Catholic immigration, the founding of Mormonism, and the need to respond educationally to a society growing increasingly urban. It might be argued that one element of immigration, of the rise of Mormonism, and of the openness to urbanization is made up of numerous individual decisions, and that would be correct. It is also the case that the United States has always had a relatively "unregulated religious economy" (Finke and Stark 1992:17–21), which allowed persons considerable leeway in making those decisions. But to assert, as I do here, that the shift toward greater governmental neutrality toward religion has been structural and the inevitable consequence of other changes in American society does not re-quire the denial of all personal—in this case, religious—influences in the process. It does mean, however, that the process whereby separation re-places accommodation occurs whether or not pro-religious or anti-religious forces are involved; such religious influence will be, at most, indirect.

This point can be made by a close analogy from the history of higher ed-ucation in America. Consider the following from George M. Marsden's *The Soul of the American University* (1994:4):

As late as 1870 the vast majority of these [nineteenth-century American colleges] were remarkably evangelical. Most of them had clergymen-presidents who taught courses defending biblicist Christianity and who encouraged periodic campus revivals. Yet within half a century the uni-versities that emerged from these evangelical colleges, while arguably carrying forward the spirit of their evangelical forebears, had become conspicuously inhospitable to the letter of such evangelicalism. By the 1920s the evangelical Protestantism of the old-time colleges had been ef-fectively excluded from leading university classrooms.

This change, it is clear, was not the change aimed for but instead arose as the unintended consequence of other aims. Marsden himself says that "once a college or university makes a commitment to serve primarily the whole public, it acquires obligations to a wide variety of constituencies and even-tually is shaped in the image of those constituencies" (1994:443, n.20).

Something comparable happened in the understanding and application of the Religion Clauses: What constituted "the whole public" in the legal realm underwent redefinition, and government became more and more neutral toward religion as separation underwent a process of replacing ac-commodation, a process still occurring. Borrowing a felicitous metaphor from Max Weber's analysis of "rationalization" (see, e.g., Gerth and Mills

1946), I am viewing this process of change as a train going along a track. The track has periodic switching stations, which, depending on the directional choice made, commits the train to one course and effectively prohibits its ever returning to the other course. Thus a choice made at one time influences the options that later present themselves.

This historical viewpoint offers a perspective lying somewhere between unrestrained cultural relativism, on the one hand, and hidebound determinism—whether materialist or idealist—on the other. Many factors account for the general direction and speed of the train, so to speak, factors that may or may not be subject to human influence, but at certain points human decisions are made that thereafter have impact on the train's course. The train is neither free to reverse its direction (as implied in radical relativism) nor does it merely follow a pattern inexorably laid down in advance (as implied in radical determinism).

I follow this model in the remaining pages of chapter 2 and in chapters 3 and 4.

How Separation Began in America

As much as some citizens may have wished that *their* church be established by the new American federal government, there was, it seems, no chance of that. Because of their numbers, Congregationalists in New England and Episcopalians in the South would alone have been able to veto one another and thus all other denominations. More to the point, perhaps, interested persons were able to retain the tepid church establishments the individual states had until such time as disestablishment seemed indicated. If Massachusetts exemplifies the general situation, such disestablishment was indicated when the complications of religious pluralism became clear. Charles H. Lippy has done an instructive job analyzing the Massachusetts Constitutional Convention from this perspective. The convention met in 1779–1780 to write, among other provisions, an Article 3 authorizing towns "to make suitable provision, at their own expense, for the institution of publick worship of God, and for the support and maintenance of publick

Protestant Teachers of piety, religion, and morality" (1978:538). Though Article 3 was ratified after much public debate, the resulting "establish-ment"—often noted as the last to be disestablished in 1833—turned out not to be much of an establishment at all. Lippy (1978:548) asks rhetorically:

> Even if it [Article 3] did not grant de jure establishment to any single re-ligious group, did it actually provide de facto establishment to the domi-nant Congregationalism? One perspective comes from the numerous court cases brought by Baptists and others against various towns between 1780 and 1800 when legislation made exemption . . . easier. Interestingly, no statewide suits were filed, but all were based on specific incidents . . . in particular towns. . . . Most often, but not always, decisions went in fa-vor of dissenters. . . . Other cases raised less readily resolvable questions. Was an itinerant minister eligible to receive state funds? Was a Roman Catholic priest eligible? Did a group have to be legally incorporated be-fore its teachers could receive subsidy? What determined whether a group constituted a sect sufficiently distinct from others in its area to warrant separate incorporation? The simple fact that these issues were raised sug-gests that legal establishment of a specific religion never occurred.

Something of the Massachusetts experience is no doubt to be found in the other twelve original states. In North Carolina, for example, the Church of England had founded missions throughout the eighteenth century, and An-glicanism had thus achieved legally established status. However, by the time of the Revolutionary War, Anglicans (because of links to the English Crown) not only had fallen out of favor but were outnumbered by Baptists. The lat-ter led the opposition to an established church of any kind, a feature put into the state's constitution in 1776 (Lefler 1973:134–40). These experiences suggest that forces for church-state separation and government neutrality to-ward religion were at work from the very beginning of the American nation.

The Process of Separation

Disestablishment of the sort just described represented a real departure from the model of church-state fusion then prevailing in Europe. It did not immediately signify a rejection of America's Christian heritage, however. We have already seen that the influential Justice Story operated as if Protestantism were merely a synonym for all that is ethical. Indeed, so readily was the evangelical "Christian-ness" of America assumed that it was only after the Civil War that the first legal decision explicitly denied claims that Christianity was part of the common law (*Board of Education v. Minor* [1872], cited by political scientist H. Frank Way). The circumstances were these: In Cincinnati, Ohio, Catholics had gained such political strength that they could effectively threaten to vote against public school bonds if the Protestant Bible readings in the tax-supported schools were not stopped. As a result, the Board of Education called a halt to the long-standing practice, which led to a lawsuit to reverse the Board's decision, a lawsuit that then went to the Ohio Supreme Court. As Way notes (1987:520):

> The decision of the Ohio Supreme Court, upholding the Board's order, was path-breaking. It not only abandoned the Christian communitarian mode of analysis, it attacked the Christian framework as singularly inappropriate . . . , noting that the state can have no religious opinion.

This decision, Way continues, "marked the first fully secular judicial rationale for religious liberty. What the Ohio court realized was that in a religiously diverse society, the state and all its agencies must be secular" (Way 1987:520; see also Michaelsen 1970:89–98 for a fuller discussion of this case).

Way's comments are contained in an article published in the *Journal of Church and State* entitled "The Death of the Christian Nation." The article leaves no doubt about the correctness of this section's thesis; from its beginning the United States has moved from greater accommodation to less and from less governmental neutrality toward religion to more. Evidence offered by Way is organized into five categories of dispute: (1) Sabbath closing laws, (2) public school prayer and Bible reading, (3) blasphemy cases, (4) public aid to sectarian schools, and (5) ownership of church property. Between 1800 and 1920, Way found records of 254 decisions, most taking place in a state's highest appellate court.

Bible Reading

We have already looked at the 1872 decision by the Ohio Supreme Court, which, for that state, outlawed Bible reading. This principle, of course, did not reach the national level until 1963, when the U.S. Supreme Court struck down Pennsylvania's requirement that "at least ten verses from the Holy Bible be read, without comment, at the opening of each public school on each school day" (*Abington Township v. Schempp*). It is nonetheless true that between 1872 and 1963 a number of states had also come to Ohio's decision—Wisconsin in 1890, Nebraska in 1902, Illinois in 1910.

What makes clear the significance of such changes when they did occur are earlier cases, when governments were *not* neutral. In 1854 the Maine Supreme Court upheld the expulsion of a Roman Catholic student for her refusal to participate in Protestant exercises. Something similar occurred in the Boston public schools, where the beating of Catholic students for not participating in religious exercises was upheld. In other words, what was challenged in Ohio in 1872 had been earlier accepted by much of the population and judiciary alike: The King James Bible was not thought to be sectarian but a book of profound moral teaching and thus in principle acceptable to all; accepted by the vast majority, it was proper for government to accommodate required Bible reading.

Blasphemy

Accommodation is also found in the blasphemy cases, cases of persons who expressed contempt for Christianity. In the early decades of the nation's history such persons were punished on the grounds that, while they were certainly free to express the "christianity" (often written in lower case in this context) they preferred, they were not free to undermine the morality derived from christianity and thus the sanctity of oaths and ultimately the peace and safety of society. In due time, however, such cases ceased to appear on the courts' dockets.

Sunday Closing

Cases involving Sabbath closing laws illustrate yet another way by which separation overtakes accommodation. Laws that kept the Sabbath holy were minimally disruptive in a largely Protestant community with a small-scale political economy. With the advent of the factory, the railroad and telegraph, and refrigeration, however, pressures mounted to allow commercial activity on Sundays. The point here is that however much Jews, Seventh-day Adventists, and other Saturday worshipers were inconvenienced, structural forces largely beyond governmental control helped get rid of Sabbath closing laws. More subtly, as Way notes, along the way even the judicial rationale for upholding those closing laws that were upheld underwent a change—from the basis of America's being a Christian nation to the basis of the need for a common day of rest. The claim by Himmelfarb cited earlier in this chapter—that vestiges of Christianity remain— is nicely illustrated at this juncture; in *Braunfeld v. Brown* (1961), the U.S. Supreme Court allowed to stand a Pennsylvania law prohibiting the sale of certain goods on Sunday, on the grounds not that this is a Christian nation but to provide a day that, "as best possible, eliminates the atmosphere of commercial noise and activity."

Catholics

Roman Catholics posed an especially difficult challenge to the assumed Protestant Christianity of America. Present from the beginning but in relative small numbers, Catholics came in massive waves of immigration starting early in the nineteenth century. Most of the church-state challenge came in the realm of education and dealt with Bible reading, as we have observed, but challenge also centered around the honoring of Catholic holidays in public schools as well as requested tax support in some form for parochial schools.

This challenge continues to this day, though of course on very different grounds. Tax money can buy textbooks for use in Catholic parochial schools, for example, but only for secular subjects; likewise, government may fund the costs of buildings on Catholic college campuses, but not if anything religious is to occur in them. What is and is not permissible, in other words, is still open to debate. What is not permissible any longer is a decision that favors Protestants at the expense of Catholics because of the assumption that "this nation is based on christianity."

Just how difficult that lesson was to learn is exemplified in a 1922 decision by the Georgia Supreme Court in a case of Bible reading that was challenged by some citizens of Rome, Georgia. Among other provisions on which they based their challenge was the Georgia Constitution, which denied tax money to "any sectarian institution." They claimed that reading from the King James Bible and not from the Catholic Douay Bible was thus a constitutional violation. Not so, said the Court, and gave three reasons:

1. Differences between the two versions of the Bible are "not known to the ordinary lay reader."
2. Although tax-supported teachers lead the exercises, they teach the "creed of no sect."
3. The "real object" of the No Establishment Clause is "to exclude all rivalry among Christian sects," and the King James Bible, while different from the Douay, is not anti-Roman Catholic.

The insight that came to the Ohio justices in 1872 had not yet reached Georgia in 1922. (The case is further analyzed in Hammond 1984.)

Church Property Disputes

H. Frank Way's fifth category of cases involves instances where courts have been called upon to resolve disputes over which faction of a congregation rightfully owns church property. There is little in these cases that *directly* reflects the Religion Clauses, but that makes the category all the more instructive for Way's argument about "the death of the Christian nation," which is my thesis in this chapter. Surprisingly, nearly half of Way's 254 cases fall into this category, indicating how fractious Protestants can be.

Overwhelmingly the disputes involved doctrine and polity, and initially the courts relied on a congregation's majority vote to decide the issue. But "Beginning in the 1830s the courts . . . adopted an implied trust rule. . . . It is this rule, the so-called Pearson rule, which casts a long and revealing shadow on American church-state relations" (Way 1987:525). The Pearson rule was that, in divisions over doctrine and polity, the property should be awarded to that part of the church, no matter how small, that was judged most "faithful" to the group's "original doctrine and polity." Not until *Watson v. Jones* (1872) was the constitutionality of this procedure questioned, so for half a century, as Way says, "civil courts . . . acted as ecclesiastical courts, often judging the merits of complex theological issues" (1987:527). Only if judges felt confident that they knew the "original doctrine and polity" of a group could they continue in this practice of preference and discrimination. They did not regard religious neutrality as their obligation, nor was state to remain separate from church, at least not as long as America still showed signs of being a Christian nation. But that practice, too, came to a halt.

Additional Support

I have borrowed from H. Frank Way's article in support of this chapter's thesis because he offers compelling evidence in its favor. So, however, does Robert T. Handy in *A Christian America* and in *Undermined Establishment*. The latter book is especially enlightening in its focus on those decades when final hopes for a "Christian America" were being dashed by realities that no longer could be ignored. Before the Civil War, evangelical Protestantism still prevailed in many parts of the United States, but after World War I none but the naive still thought a "Christian America" was constitutional or even possible. Of course, such realization did not stop all efforts in that direction, then or now.

Jews, Turks, and Infidels by Morton Borden is another excellent survey of the challenges to the implied Christian character of the United States, including a counter-challenge in 1864 and ensuing years by the National Reform Association. This was an organization devoted to the aim of amending the U.S. Constitution to recognize "the rulership of Jesus Christ and the supremacy of the divine law" (Borden 1984:62).

Of course, by now such an aim is probably recognized as unrealistic by everyone, though that does not stop some modest efforts in the same direction even today. Most Americans, however, place high value on religious liberty and, when forced by circumstances to confront the implications of safeguarding that liberty, they acknowledge that accommodating Protestant Christianity, and thus accommodating any religion, is contrary to the American church-state code. Even accommodating *all* religions raises profound issues, as we shall see in chapters 3 and 4. Structural features of modern-day America—especially religious pluralism and government's inevitable involvement in our lives—ordains a secular state and an increasingly separationist stance by the courts.

Conclusion

Why, then, do books such as Richard John Neuhaus's *The Naked Public Square,* calling for more religion in more places of public life, or Stephen Carter's *The Culture of Disbelief,* calling for more weight given to religion in public debate, become best-sellers? How can fundamentalist Protestants seriously propose a constitutional amendment to allow state-sponsored prayer in public schools and find significant support even among those whose own prayers might be the first to be excluded? What does it mean when, in a Supreme Court case that ruled school-sponsored prayer unconstitutional yet again, Justice Scalia, joined by fellow Justices Rehnquist, Thomas, and White, dissented (*Lee v. Weisman* [1992])? The answer to all these questions is, of course, that the law is not as settled in all aspects of church-state relations as this chapter might suggest. It bears repeating that I have argued not that church-state matters are settled but that the direction of change in how those matters get settled is discernible. That direction is from accommodation to separation, from religious toleration to religious liberty. It was his belief that this is the direction of change that led legal scholar Marvin E. Frankel, an avowed separationist, to predict (1994:12) that Scalia's dissent in *Lee v. Weisman* stands a good chance of being the high-water mark of the minority attempt to extinguish ideas of separation and government neutrality that the Court has enforced with only occasional slippage since 1947. In both style and substance, the opinion exhibits an impatient distaste for deviant sensibilities getting in the way of majority preferences—which is, very broadly speaking, what the First Amendment is for.

In other words, Justice Scalia and others sharing his viewpoint are out of step with the direction of change in American legal decision making. I agree, but I want to make the case in much more detail, and separately, for Free Exercise and No Establishment. Those discussions constitute chapters 3 and 4.

3

THE FREE EXERCISE CLAUSE: FROM RELIGIOUS TOLERATION TO RELIGIOUS LIBERTY

In the Introduction to this book I quoted Mark DeWolfe Howe's assertion that the Framers aimed at "converting the liberal principle of tolerance into the radical principle of liberty." This latter phrase I take to mean the recognition that it is individual conscience that deserves protection under the First Amendment. While not every student of the Constitution-writing period would agree with Howe's assertion, all would agree that, if such was indeed the Framers' "aim," reaching the target has been a long time happening. Even now, as we saw at the end of chapter 2, some extremists among the accommodationists think that the "liberal principle of tolerance" is all that was intended and all, therefore, that should be constitutionally mandated now.

Here in chapter 3 my purpose is not to argue whether or not the original intent was indeed to protect conscience rather than guarantee toleration. First, I have no warrant for trying to adjudicate a two-hundred-year-old debate. Second, however, from the standpoint of this book, the Framers' *intent* is of less importance than the *succession of interpretations* of that intent, the decisions that connect their era with our own, a succession of events in which a series of decision makers at least believed themselves to be following the original intent of the Constitution in a changing world. Thus, just as certain things occurred before the writing of the First Amendment that influenced that writing—such things as the English Toleration Act and John Locke's *Letters Concerning Toleration*—so have other things occurred since 1789 that have influenced how the First Amendment is understood and applied. Thus David A. J. Richards's judgment can be correct in declaring Locke's *Letters* "classically authoritative for the

Anglo-American democratic tradition" (1986:89), without our having to know just how many of the Framers were influenced by them. It is enough to find in the First Amendment itself the germ of the idea of a protected conscience, and then to find in the path of that amendment's interpretation a discernible pattern of unfolding concern to protect that conscience. In this way is the train-on-a-track metaphor helpful.

We know, for example, that James Madison, one of the architects of Virginia's 1776 Declaration of Rights and author of the 1785 Memorial and Remonstrance (opposing Virginia's General Assessment Bill), referred in those documents to the "free exercise of religion" according to the dictates of "conscience." Not surprisingly, Madison retained the word "conscience" in reworking the various renderings that resulted in the First Amendment. It is true that by the eighth version of that Amendment, the word "conscience" was dropped and did not reappear in the tenth and final version (Malbin, 1978:22–26), but it is doubtful that, as Stanley Ingber contends (1989:252), the dropping of the word shows that the Framers meant something distinctively different by the words "conscience" and "religion." Indeed, of the thirteen states that had constitutions in place before the adoption of the Bill of Rights, nine used the word "conscience" in their sections dealing with religion, typically in phrasing to the effect that religion was free to be practiced "according to the dictates of conscience." Of the thirty-five states that joined the Union between 1789 and 1912, when New Mexico and Arizona were added, only seven (20 percent) *failed* to use the word "conscience" in the religion sections of their constitutions. Not until Alaska and Hawaii became states in 1959 do we find the wording of the federal constitution essentially duplicated in their state constitutions. Conscience, therefore, might even be said to have been the preferred label for whatever American citizens wanted to protect in the sacred sphere.

But, Ingber goes on to say (1989:252), this deletion of "conscience" in the final version of the First Amendment

> is easily explained if the framers had any inkling that a right to conscience might suggest that philosophical and personal beliefs, as well as religious beliefs, could justify claims of exemption from laws of general

applicability under the free exercise clause. Such an implication would have been totally inconsistent with the liberal democratic theory popular at the time.

Since, as I hope to show in this chapter, the Free Exercise Clause *is* now more or less interpreted in just the way Ingber believes would horrify the Framers, it is not an insignificant matter to wonder whether such an interpretation is indeed "totally inconsistent" with democratic theory at the time. I want to suggest it is not.

Ingber may be correct with respect to most of the Framers, but apparently not all. Especially in Jefferson and Madison do we see evidence that they favored not just religious tolerance but, more radically, an inviolate conscience. What is the difference? According to David Richards—who would agree with Ingber had Ingber not said "totally" inconsistent—the two Virginians' commitment to religious liberty, as distinct from mere toleration, represented a "sharp departure" from the Western political tradition. With Lockean inspiration, then, Jefferson and Madison perceived that central to the religious issue is a question more profound than how many religious perspectives will be recognized and how different they can be. Behind or under the question of toleration was the question of equality. And true equality calls for the presumption of "rational freedom," which, as Richards says (1986:85), amounts to everyone's "inalienable right to conscience."

Of course, what was meant by conscience in the eighteenth century was not what is meant today. Probably most Americans at the time, including those who wrote and voted on the First Amendment, imagined most "consciences" to be "Christian" and saw the "free exercise" provision as a guarantee that people could express their Christianity in whatever manner they wanted. Nonetheless, more than Christian conscience was of concern; indeed, more than theism. As Derek Davis says, "Some of the founders clearly sought religious freedom for non-theists" (1993:92). Therefore, while the core element in persons that animates and compels them was conceived differently then from the way it is conceived today, it is clear that at least some Framers wanted special treatment for that core element. As

Milton Konvitz puts it, it was "perfectly natural" for Thomas Jefferson to write, in a letter to Edward Dowse in 1803, "'We are bound, you, I and every one, to make common cause . . . to maintain the common right of freedom of conscience'"(Konvitz 1968:87).

So ardent indeed was Jefferson about "freedom of conscience" that his support for free exercise took on an anti-church character. Since freedom of conscience was, for him, an inalienable right, its formation and development must be subject to no government, and therefore government must give support to no church lest it contaminate that freedom (Richards 1986:147).

If this interpretation is correct, Jefferson was not so concerned that state aid to religion would "advance the interest of impious clerks," as Howe puts it (1965:19), but instead shared with evangelicals the concern that the "wilderness" of government not invade the "garden" of religion. And Jefferson's concept of that garden was larger than most.

It is true, of course, that Jefferson was generally critical of churches because of the authority claimed by their leaders, reserving his admiration for Quakers because they renounced priests and bishops (Wills 1990:359). But that is precisely the point; Jefferson wanted constitutional protection for the human element he called conscience, an element commonly—though not always—couched in religious terms. Jefferson would protect that element, however couched.

While probably nobody at the time would have articulated the matter this way, those favoring liberty of conscience over mere toleration were creating a perspective in which *conviction,* rather than the *substance* of the conviction, was to be honored. It was not to be *what* a person felt compelled to do, or *why* a person felt compelled, but the *fact of compulsion* that deserved special treatment.

I am not asserting, then, that the Framers really foresaw the concept of free exercise that would emerge in the second half of the twentieth century. I am claiming, however, that one can find in the words of some key persons at the time the kernel of a doctrine of protected conscience that would develop in response to subsequent events into the notion of free exercise we have today. We turn now to some of those events.

Strategic Events on
the Path of Free Exercise

The U.S. Constitution requires of the Supreme Court only that it decide cases, not that it render reasons for its decisions. Given the importance of precedent in Anglo-American law, however, it is clear why, from the beginning, the Court has provided often elaborate justifications for its decisions. Not only are these justifications meant to explain to the losing side why it lost; in addition, everyone else is instructed about what will and will not be legal in similar cases.

The Supreme Court, however, deals only with cases that work their way to it. It has discretion in which cases it will hear, and therefore it can wait until a case comes along that exhibits a constitutional issue the Court wants to clarify, but it cannot reach out to decide just any issue. This limitation on the Supreme Court is important here because it means that, until the adoption of the Fourteenth Amendment after the Civil War, which bit by bit extended U.S. constitutional rights into every state, the Supreme Court had cases coming largely from U.S. territories, which were not yet states. Its religion cases were few and far between.

Religiously Motivated Action

One notable case was *Reynolds v. United States* (1879). Reynolds was a Mormon with two wives living in the Utah territory. The U.S. Congress, which had jurisdiction over Utah, had passed a law making plural marriages in U.S. territories illegal, and Reynolds challenged that law. He lost, but what makes the case noteworthy is the fact that for the first time the Supreme Court employed the so-called "belief–action" distinction. The distinction was common enough even in colonial times, but now it became constitutional doctrine. The idea is simple: the Free Exercise Clause gives absolute freedom to *believe* as one chooses, but *actions* reflecting those beliefs are subject to government restraint. "Congress was deprived of all legislative power over mere opinion," wrote Chief Justice Waite, "but was left free to reach actions which were in violation of social duties or subversive of good order." The Court claimed that polygamy was indeed destructive of good order and therefore upheld the law in the face of Reynolds's challenge.

The belief–action distinction operated pretty much unchanged until 1940. Laws could be passed regulating behavior, and, as long as *religious* behavior was not specifically targeted, courts found such laws constitutional. In 1940, however, in *Cantwell v. Connecticut,* the Supreme Court reversed the conviction of a Jehovah's Witness who was clearly violating a breach-of-the-peace ordinance by playing in public a religious message on a portable phonograph. It was, in fact, a strongly anti–Roman Catholic message in a predominantly Roman Catholic neighborhood. Until 1940, courts would have rendered a guilty verdict—as the lower court did in this case—noting simply that it was a secular regulation being violated, a regulation that did not target Jehovah's Witnesses, or any religious group, but was applicable to all citizens.

In *Cantwell* the Supreme Court reversed the lower court's verdict, acknowledging that *religiously* motivated behavior can be constitutionally protected even though the same behavior, otherwise motivated, is not. It is important to note here that not only was the belief–action distinction being amended, but also—since obviously *some* religiously motivated actions are impermissible (for example, human sacrifice at the sacred altar) even as others are allowable—the Court had now to find some way to balance the interest on both sides of disputed actions.

In *Cantwell* the Court used the "clear and present danger" test used in free speech cases, finding that Cantwell represented no such danger. Over the next quarter century, however, a different test emerged, becoming regularized as the so-called "Sherbert test," because it was made explicit in a 1963 case, *Sherbert v. Verner.* In that case the Court found that denying a Seventh-day Adventist unemployment compensation because she refused to work on Saturday and thus got fired was an unconstitutional limitation on her free exercise of religion.

As might be imagined, and can be seen clearly in retrospect, between *Cantwell* in 1940 and *Sherbert* in 1963 the Supreme Court was struggling with other free-exercise cases in which it faced the difficult question of *which* religious actions are entitled to special protection. As Justice Douglas wrote in one of these cases, "the rights with which we are dealing are not absolutes." Not by accident, many of the cases were brought by Cantwell's fellow Jehovah's Witnesses. Could Witnesses be obliged to pay the tax that other "salesmen" paid in order to sell their religious literature? In 1942 the decision was Yes, by a vote of 5–4 (*Jones v. Opelika*). The following year, also on a 5–4 vote, that Yes vote was changed to No (*Murdock v. Pennsylvania*).

Very similar, in formal if not substantive terms, was the question of whether requiring Jehovah's Witness students to salute the flag violated their free exercise of religion, inasmuch as Witnesses regard flag saluting as idolatrous. In 1940, on a vote of 8–1, the Court said No, their rights were not violated (*Minersville School District v. Gobitis*), but three years later, on a vote of 6–3, it said Yes, they were (*West Virginia State Board of Education v. Barnette*).

Close reading of those four cases, including dissents as well as majority opinions, establishes very clearly that the Justices, in deciding when a religious action deserves special treatment versus when it is subject to the same regulation that governs other people's actions, considered such questions as whether the regulation burdened the religious plaintiff's action and, if so, how much. They asked how important to the state was it to apply the regulation in every instance, and what would be the consequences of not doing so. And they inquired into possible alternative means the state might take to achieve a regulation's purpose without burdening the religious plaintiff. Thus, for example, in *Braunfeld v. Brown* (1961), certain Orthodox Jewish merchants claimed that the law requiring them to close down on Sundays impaired their free exercise of religion because, to remain commercially competitive, they would have to violate Orthodox law and work on Saturdays. Among the options the Court considered (and rejected) was an "alternative means" whereby the state would exempt from the Sunday closing law any person who, because of religious conviction, observed a day of rest other than Sunday.

As was stated earlier, the outcome of the deliberations in these (and other free-exercise cases) after 1940 led to the "Sherbert test," so-called because the majority opinion in *Sherbert v. Verner* is so clearly organized around certain questions that must be asked about the controversy. Justice Brennan, after introducing the facts in the case, wrote, "We turn first to the question whether the disqualification for benefits imposes any burden on the free exercise of appellant's religion" and responded that it does. He goes on. "We must next consider whether some compelling state interest . . . justifies the substantial infringement of appellant's First Amendment right" and finds none. Only if Sherbert's denial of unemployment compensation had been upheld by the Court would Brennan have gone on to ask the third question raised in *Braunfeld v. Brown:* Might the state have an alternative means of achieving its purpose without burdening Sherbert? In other cases since 1963 this third question has been added to the "burden" and "compelling interest" questions, and together they constitute the Sherbert test.

It is obvious that the mere existence of this test does not automatically render decisions, but it has lent system and continuity to subsequent cases. Generated by the *Cantwell* decision in 1940, which made ineffective the long-standing belief–action distinction and required the courts to find a basis for declaring some religiously motivated actions protected by the Free Exercise Clause while others are not, the Sherbert test has more or less become that basis. While alternative tests might be imagined, it is important to the argument here to realize that, having abandoned the belief–action distinction, the Supreme Court had no choice than to devise *some* method for deciding on the constitutionality of religiously motivated action.

Applying the Sherbert Test

The Supreme Court has had numerous occasions since 1963 to apply the balancing strategy known as the Sherbert Test. One dramatic instance — dramatic because the outcome was probably unexpected and was certainly provocative — was *Wisconsin v. Yoder* (1972). In this case, Amish parents won the right to take their children out of public school after the eighth grade, arguing that any education past that point is no longer practical but instead "worldly" and thus evil in Amish theology. Just two decades earlier, the Court, in its decision desegregating the public schools of Topeka, Kansas, had declared education one of government's most important functions. Now, in 1972, the Court sided with the Amish parents, in effect saying that the burden imposed on them by Wisconsin's compulsory school attendance until age sixteen was greater than the less-than-compelling state's interest in keeping Amish children in school an additional two years. The balancing act was obvious.

It was also obvious in a 1977 case where the religious interest lost out, though this case was decided on statutory, not constitutional, grounds. In *Trans World Airlines, Inc. v. Hardison,* an employee of the airline, whose job took place in a maintenance base that operated around the clock every day, sued for his right to take Saturdays off. As a member of the Worldwide Church of God, Hardison was a Sabbatarian. The Court ruled against him on the grounds that his job was essential, and on weekends he was the only available person on his shift who could perform it. In effect, this case found (a) Hardison's free exercise was indeed burdened, but (b) TWA had a compelling interest in keeping its operation fully staffed, and (c) no alternative method, such as paying premium wages to a substitute to work an extra day, was available.

Other cases in which the religious interest lost out could be cited, though there is no need to go into detail. For example, an Orthodox Jewish psychiatrist in the Air Force was required to remove his yarmulke while in uniform indoors; the need for esprit de corps and discipline was cited as compelling. Muslim prisoners who worked as trusties outside the prison walls were not granted the special privilege of returning to prison for noon prayers on the grounds that two sets of guards would be needed if the gang was split up, and gang morale would be jeopardized by unequal amounts of labor required of Muslim and non-Muslim. A Native American father was told that the state had a legitimate compelling interest in requiring his daughter to have a Social Security number to qualify for federal government aid programs, even though the father believed that assigning his daughter a number robbed her of her soul.

It is enough for the purposes of this chapter simply to note that a balancing act, with *Sherbert* as the model, was the way by which these cases — and others that could be cited — were decided. Irrespective of which side won, questions of burden, compelling interest, and possible alternatives by which free exercise might be less burdened were addressed and weighed. As Ronald B. Flowers, long an observer of church-state court cases, says (1994:44):

> Since 1963 the Court's view of the scope of the Free Exercise Clause, and consequently the amount of religious freedom available to the American people, has varied. For most of the period, when the "Sherbert test" was the principle for interpreting the clause, Americans enjoyed a large amount of freedom for religious practice. Those in specialized environments like the military did not enjoy the full range of this freedom, but decisions in these areas had little implication for the general population.

The Sherbert Test
Is Challenged

In 1990, in a case involving unemployment compensation for two Native Americans who had been fired after admitting they used peyote in a ceremony of the Native American Church (*Oregon Employment Division v. Smith*), the Supreme Court abandoned the "compelling interest" prong of the Sherbert test. Justice Scalia, writing for the majority, declared that Oregon's statute making peyote illegal, because it was not targeting any specific religion, was therefore applicable to all persons in the state. Moreover, the state was not even obliged to cite a compelling interest in upholding a duly legislated law.

Justice O'Connor, who voted with the majority because she thought the two employees had forfeited their right to unemployment compensation, balked at dispensing with the compelling interest criterion. She thus in part agreed with (without joining) the dissenting opinion of three other Justices, leaving a majority of five out of nine who were announcing the demise of the Sherbert test.

Court watchers and religious groups were astonished and alarmed at this turn of events. Its effect was to overturn what had become the Free Exercise Doctrine. Since *Reynolds,* government had been able to restrict religious action, but in doing so, the Court said, government was *required* to justify the restriction; now, government would have vast power to restrict religious action provided only that the restriction was not aimed specifically at religion. In his zeal to reduce the "legislative" function of the Supreme Court, Scalia had dismantled a long-developing understanding of religious liberty in the United States.

By November 1993, Congress had passed, and President Clinton had signed, the Religious Freedom Restoration Act (RFRA). The heart of the act states that government may not "substantially burden" a person's exercise of religion unless it demonstrates that application of the burden to the person (1) is in furtherance of a compelling governmental interest and (2) is the least restrictive means of furthering that compelling government interest.

It is obvious that Congress wanted the Sherbert test restored. It is just as clear that a majority of Supreme Court Justices saw RFRA as a congressional usurpation of the judicial branch's power, as we saw in the discussion of *Boerne v. Flores* in chapter 1. Ever since *Marbury v. Madison* in 1803, it is the Supreme Court that has determined the constitutionality of legislative acts.

The combination of *Smith,* RFRA, and then *Boerne v. Flores* did little to clarify free-exercise jurisprudence. The Roman Catholic Church in Boerne, Texas, had outgrown its building and wanted to expand. Its building was in a "historic zone" regulated by special rules that, the city stated, prevented the church from expanding. Archbishop Flores argued that, under RFRA, Boerne could restrict the church's expansion only if it had a compelling interest in doing so. The city responded that there was no requirement to present a compelling interest because RFRA itself was unconstitutional. In *Boerne v. Flores* the Supreme Court agreed, thus making that case more a referendum on judicial decision-making than a free-exercise question.

Until *Boerne,* the only free-exercise case before the Court was one in which the city of Hialeah, Florida, was found to have violated the religious liberty of the Church of the Lukumi Babalu Aye by enacting legislation prohibiting the sacrifice of animals. By unanimous vote, the Justices found that the legislation was directed specifically at conduct motivated by religious belief and was thus unconstitutional. In other words, no "compelling interest" question was involved. The Sherbert test is in an ambiguous position therefore.

We can hope that the Court will somehow return to the earlier prevailing view that, in Justice Jackson's words in *West Virginia v. Barnette* (the 1943 case that granted Jehovah's Witness pupils the right not to salute the U.S. flag):

> The very purpose of a Bill of Rights was to withdraw certain subjects from the vicissitudes of political controversy, to place them beyond the reach of majorities and officials and to establish them as legal principles to be applied by the courts. One's right to . . . freedom of worship . . . may not be submitted to vote; [it] depend[s] on the outcome of no elections.

What Is Religious?

The Court had, in *Cantwell* and similar cases, created another troubling question that it could not dodge: What *is* religious? If, in abandoning the belief–action distinction, the law would protect some actions only if they were religiously motivated, the law needed some way to identify what is religious. It is perhaps no coincidence that during the quarter century the Court was evolving the Sherbert test it was wrestling with this second question too. Its resolution, while conceptually clear, is, like the Sherbert test, not easily applied.

The evolution of the answer to this second question began in 1944 in *United States v. Ballard*. Guy Ballard and his family led the I AM movement, which, among other things, made claims of being able to cure diseases that doctors called incurable. These claims were made in mailings to people, asking for the payment of money in exchange for the spiritual cure. Because the U.S. Post Office was involved, the government brought suit against the Ballards, charging fraud. In effect, then, the government was saying that the I AM movement's doctrines were not true and that the Ballards knew they were not true. The trial judge, however, instructed the jury that they were to decide not whether the doctrines were true but only whether the Ballards *believed* them to be true. On that basis the defendants were acquitted, and the government appealed to the Supreme Court.

The *Ballard* case is vitally important for the story here because it argued the point that government must not get involved in determining the truth or falsity of any religion—indeed, must not even define religion. Justice Douglas, for the majority, wrote:

> Heresy trials are foreign to our Constitution. Men may believe what they cannot prove. . . . The religious views espoused by respondents might seem incredible, if not preposterous, to most people. But if those doctrines are subject to trial before a jury charged with finding their truth or falsity, then the same can be done with the religious beliefs of any sect.

As stark as the majority opinion was, Justice Jackson would have gone even further. Deciding what is or is not religion, Jackson wrote in dissent, "is precisely the thing the Constitution put beyond the reach of the prosecutor, for the price of freedom of religion or of speech or of the press is that we must put up with, and even pay for, a good deal of rubbish."

This position of the Court's neutrality with respect to the definition of religion was foreshadowed in the nineteenth-century "church property" disputes, as we saw in chapter 2. (Indeed, from *Watson v. Jones* [1872] comes the memorable phrase "The law knows no heresy.") In those cases, it will be recalled, the Justices came to see that they were behaving as an ecclesiastical court whenever they took on the task of deciding which faction in an ownership quarrel was more faithful to the church's "original" doctrine and polity. Just as the Court then decided it was exceeding its constitutional authority, so did the Court in *Ballard* conclude that it must not decide the "truth" of any religion because this would, in effect, be deciding what is and is not religion.

An uncritical reading of *United States v. Ballard* might lead to the supposition that government really must maintain a hands-off policy when it comes to defining religion. Alas, as we shall now see, that has proved to be impossible.

From Religion to Conscience

Just as the *Cantwell* decision—which found that action motivated by religion is protected but the same action otherwise motivated is not—forced onto the Supreme Court the task of identifying religious motivation, so did the *Ballard* case force onto the Court the task of determining the subject matter of the Religion Clauses. And just as the *Sherbert v. Verner* case was the symbolic accomplishment of the first task, so was the task launched by *Ballard* accomplished with a clear-cut case in 1965 (*United States v. Seeger*), in which a self-proclaimed nonreligious person was unanimously granted the status of conscientious objector to war. As with the evolution of *Cantwell* to *Sherbert,* so too with the evolution of *Ballard* to *Seeger:* A series of decisions between *Ballard* and *Seeger* can, in retrospect, be seen to have made the outcome all but inevitable.

Soon after *Ballard* the Supreme Court was asked to rule on the constitutionality of parochial school students' use of tax revenue funds to get to school by public bus (*Everson v. Board of Education* [1947]). In finding this subsidy permissible, the Court went on to say that "neither a State nor the Federal Government can constitutionally force a person to profess a belief or disbelief in any religion." The message of *Ballard*—that government may not judge the truth or falsity of any religion—was once again affirmed.

It was also affirmed when the judicial system was asked whether humanistic or nontheistic "religious" organizations were entitled to tax exemption. Members of such groups looked upon them as the equivalent of churches, often meeting on Sundays to sing hymns, hear sermons, and take up collections of money. Were they not also eligible for tax exemption? In 1957, in *Fellowship of Humanity v. County of Alameda,* an appellate court ruled that such groups are entitled to the same tax exemption given to ordinary churches. To deny them that privilege, the California court said, would be to favor theism over nontheism, something clearly prohibited because it required a judgment about the *content* of belief. Instead, stated the court, the judgment should be based on the belief's *function*—"whether or not the belief occupies the same place in the lives of its holders that . . . orthodox beliefs occupy in the lives of believing majorities."

In 1961 the Supreme Court faced another kind of issue in which the state's authority to impose religious (or irreligious) belief was questioned. A year earlier, the Maryland Court of Appeals, the highest court in that state, had upheld the denial of a notary public commission for Roy R. Torcaso (*Torcaso v. Watkins* [1960]) because he refused to declare a belief in God as required by Maryland's constitution for positions of "profit or trust." Among other justifications for its decision, the court noted that

> to the members of the [Maryland Constitutional] Convention, as to the voters who adopted our [State] Constitution, belief in God was equated with a belief in moral accountability and the sanctity of an oath. We may assume that there may be permissible differences in the individual's conception of God. But it seems clear that under our [State] Constitution disbelief in a Supreme Being, and the denial of any moral accountability for conduct, not only renders a person incompetent to hold public office, but to give testimony, or serve as a juror. The historical record makes it clear that religious toleration, in which the State has taken pride, was never thought to encompass the ungodly.

This decision, hardly out of step with many nineteenth-century cases we encountered in chapter 2, was overturned by the U.S. Supreme Court the following year in *Torcaso v. Watkins* (1961). The Court was following the logic declared in *Ballard, Everson,* and other cases—the logic that, in the ringing words of Justice Jackson quoted earlier, "The very purpose of the Bill of Rights was to withdraw certain subjects from the vicissitudes of political controversy."

In each of these cases we see the Supreme (or other) Court concluding that what once was *not* entitled to special treatment now *is,* which is to say that what *constitutes* religion has undergone considerable expansion. Nothing illustrates this expansion better than the 1965 *Seeger* case, and, five years later, *Welsh v. United States,* a case nearly identical to *Seeger.*

Conscientious objection has long been recognized in American law. At one point, membership in a so-called "peace church" (often Mennonite or Quaker) determined one's eligibility for that status, but over the years eligibility rules loosened somewhat in recognition of the great variety of religious beliefs found in the United States. In 1948, Congress amended the Selective Service Act again, declaring that, for the purposes of draft boards, eligibility would be determined by one's

> religious training and belief [which] means an individual's belief in a relation to a Supreme Being involving duties superior to those arising from any human relation, but does not include essentially political, sociological, or philosophical views or a merely personal moral code (50 United States Code App. ¶456 [j] 1958 ed.).

In the 1965 case, Seeger contended that, though he did not believe in a Supreme Being, he did have a "faith in a purely ethical creed" and thus was entitled to conscientious objector status. The Supreme Court agreed. His creed, the Justices said, was the equivalent of a religion, which they characterized in the phrase a "sincere and meaningful belief which occupies in the life of its possessor a place parallel to that filled by the God of those admittedly qualifying for the exemption," virtually the same wording found in *Fellowship of Humanity v. County of Alameda.* Five years later, in *Welsh,* the majority opinion went even further in declaring eligible for exemption from military service "all those whose consciences, spurred by deeply held moral, ethical, or religious beliefs, would give no rest or peace if they allowed themselves to become a part of an instrument of war." The Court, as one legal scholar put it some years later (Ingber 1989:260), left "no room for any residual doubt." It "viewed deeply and sincerely held moral or ethical beliefs as the functional, and thus the legal, equivalent of religious beliefs. The Justices had obfuscated any distinction between religion and all other belief systems."

Three Justices dissented in *Welsh,* suggesting something less than unanimity on exactly how conscientious objection cases are to be decided. But if the argument here is correct, even if *Seeger* and *Welsh* did not establish the principle that "conscience" is now the legal equivalent of "religion," those cases provide a reasonable basis for assuming that it is only a matter of time before it will be. Richards (1986:131) states the case well:

> Such cases suggest the guarantee of religious free exercise might encompass freedom of conscience as such. While the Supreme Court has

drawn back from embracing any such clear statement of principle, the gravitational pull to this principle in the case law is obvious, and it may be the most just interpretation of underlying constitutional principles.

As early as 1919, Harlan Fiske Stone, later Justice and then Chief Justice of the Supreme Court (and a dissenter in *Ballard!*), wrote (1919:263), "While conscience is commonly associated with religious convictions, all experience teaches us that the supreme moral imperative which sometimes actuates men to choose one course of action in preference to another and to adhere to it at all costs may be dissociated from what is commonly recognized as religious experience."

In 1943, in *United States v. Kauten,* a Federal District Court exempted an atheist from the draft on the grounds that

> a conscience which categorically requires the believer to disregard elementary self-interest and to accept martyrdom in preference to transgressing its tenets . . . may justly be regarded as a response of the individual to an inward mentor, call it conscience or God, that is for many persons at the present time the equivalent of what has always been thought a religious impulse.

Given this unfolding of interpretations, how could conscience *not* eventually be recognized as the equivalent of religion? Such recognition came about not from mere changes in court personnel or mere volition on the part of those personnel. Rather, it resulted from pressures that mounted in America's history and social structure. At least two of these were massively influential: (1) increased religious pluralism, and (2) increased government regulation—and thus intrusion—in citizens' lives, including their religious lives. When the First Amendment was drafted, religious freedom was guaranteed and everyone "knew" what religion was. Free exercise meant absolute freedom of belief, but religious behavior could be regulated as long as the Establishment Clause was not violated through differential treatment of religions. However, religious freedom came to be seen as honoring religiously motivated behavior, which meant that identifying what was truly religious became necessary. And *that* was seen as casting judges as "theologians," clearly an unconstitutional role.

For these reasons, the point was reached in judicial operations where questions of what and how religion was practiced no longer mattered; instead, questions about sincerity and fervor were asked. In other words, it was the *fact* of conviction, not the *content* of that conviction, that the First Amendment was understood to protect. Free exercise now referred to *conscience,* whether articulated in religious language or not. (This argument is variously addressed in Carmela 1993, Davis 1993, Frankel 1994, Galanter 1966, Greenawalt 1993, Ingber 1989, and Lerner 1989.)

The Loss That Comes with Gain

Milton R. Konvitz makes this argument in very strong terms. He speculates (1968:99) on how church-state history would be different had the Framers worded the Religion Clauses to protect the "free exercise of conscience":

> This enlargement would have saved us much trouble. We would not have needed to worry over whether Ethical Culture or humanism is a religion, or whether the pacifism of a Seeger . . . is based on a religious belief. For at the heart of the beliefs of such men and movements is conscience, and persons who avow religious beliefs . . . do not hold a monopoly on conscience.

This last thought is profound indeed: If religious beliefs are anchored in conscience, it is conscience that is primary and religion its possible derivative. In this perspective, as I will explore more fully in chapter 6, religion is the *language* of conscience, but persons need not use a particular language in order to make claims of conscience. As Konvitz perceives, before *Seeger* and *Welsh* the Supreme Court had, in effect, insisted that conscience "must speak as religion if it is to be heard in the legal forum" (1968:104). Or, as Justice Harlan wrote in a concurring opinion in *Welsh,* "The constitutional question . . . is whether a statute that defers to the individual's conscience only when his views emanate from adherence to theistic religious beliefs is within the power of Congress."

Apparently Congressman Ronald V. Dellums of California thinks not. In 1992 he introduced HR5060, Military Conscientious Objector Act of 1992, which would recognize "sincerely held moral, ethical, or religious beliefs" as a basis for a claim to conscientious objector status (Moskos and Chambers 1993:44). While Dellums's bill is not yet enacted, its eventual passage does appear likely, inasmuch as the rest of the modern world is also recognizing what Moskos and Chambers call the shift from "sacred to secular resistance." They cite a number of European countries, plus Australia, Israel, and South Africa, where so-called secular conscientious objection is recognized.

Ironically, reservations about this development are expressed from an unexpected quarter: historic peace churches. Although the size of this objection is unknown, it will, in the long run, be ineffective. Nonetheless, analysis of the objection does offer an opportunity to explore a far more pervasive consequence of the constitutional recognition of the rights of conscience.

Moskos and Chambers describe a 1989 interdenominational and international conference on conscientious objection where the keynote speaker, a member of a peace church (Church of the Brethren), complained that the World Council of Churches, in its policy statement regarding the conscientious objector, or CO, seemed to "legitimate conscientious objection more from a secular human rights perspective than from the Judeo-Christian imperative." The CO status, he went on, was "reduced to an individual state of distress and the foundation of the New Testament was disregarded" (quoted in Moskos and Chambers 1993:200).

Now it might seem odd that a member of a church, one of whose central tenets is pacifism, would object to enlarging the numbers of persons entitled to have their pacifism recognized. From another perspective, however, a peace church loses something as nonmembers of peace churches win: the special recognition, even the quasi-"establishment" status, it once had in society's interpretation of religious liberty. That loss can obviously be painful if only the loss, and not the gain, is perceived.

Consider the similar complaint of Richard John Neuhaus in his book *The Naked Public Square* (1984:80):

As time went on . . . the court's references to religion had less and less to do with what is usually meant by religion. That is, religion no longer referred to those communal traditions of ultimate beliefs and practice ordinarily called religion. Religion, in the court's meaning, became radically individualized and privatized. Religion became a synonym for conscience. . . . Thus religion is no longer a matter of content but of sincerity. It is no longer a matter of communal values but of individual conviction. In short, it is no longer a public reality and therefore cannot interfere with public business.

Stephen Carter is likewise confounded:

The message of contemporary culture seems to be that it is perfectly all right to believe that stuff—we have freedom of conscience, folks can believe what they like—but you really ought to keep it to yourself, especially if your beliefs are the sort that cause you to act in ways that are . . . well . . . a bit unorthodox (1993:25).

One wonders if Carter could read those words aloud to Seeger or Welsh. Would he really sacrifice their rights of conscience in exchange for a restored privileged voice for "religion"?

What many have come to understand, as Neuhaus and Carter apparently have not, is that recognizing the rights of conscience *requires* a level verbal playing field. Conscientious claims, whether stated in religious or other terms, are equal, and adjudicating among those claims *requires* a language all can use meaningfully. Thus, what Neuhaus sees as a "naked public square"—the exclusion of religion from the conduct of public business—means merely the devaluation of religious language in public political deliberation (1984:vii). It by no means excludes conscience, whether religiously conceived or not. (I develop this point in chapter 6.)

Ralph Lerner (1989:88–89) understands how something is lost even as something is gained:

[A]s far as federal constitutional law was concerned, the focus of attention was to be shifted from groups to individuals, from sects to consciences. The new enlightened regime . . . made a new world safe, not for church or chapel or synagogue, but for each and every believer, indeed for each and every person's private conscience. . . . American society under the Constitution was open to all kinds of voluntary associations, and

. . . religionists who meant to enjoy the benefits of that regime had to quietly accept their place as one kind of association among many. Those unable to bear this muting of their clarion call would soon discover that society was equally uncomfortable with them. . . . Eschewing any pretensions to holiness or divine direction, this system of secular, enlightened indifference is large enough and generous enough to shield almost any kind of holiness so long as it minds its civil manners.

It is in minding its "civil manners," so to speak, that religion only appears to fade from view in the public square. Or, as *The New Yorker* editorialized soon after the assassination of Yitzhak Rabin, "Life in Israel today makes one long for a naked public square: Politics without God, without myth and fantasy, without eternal enemies, without sacred causes or holy ground" (November 20, 1995). The example may be extreme, but it's pertinent. A naked public square is the price paid in recognizing everyone's conscience.

Conclusion

As has been shown, a "naked public square" displeases some, even as others rejoice in such expanded religious liberty. Regardless of the response, however, this outcome had a certain kind of inevitability, as I have tried to argue in this chapter—an inevitability not in the sense of being foreordained but in the sense of necessarily evolving out of solutions to dilemmas created by earlier decisions. Chief among these decisions was *Cantwell,* which determined that some religiously motivated actions are protected by the Free Exercise Clause, thus forcing courts to develop criteria for discerning *which* actions are protected and which motivations are *religious.* As a result, religious liberty has come to include the free exercise of conscience, whether articulated religiously or not. For America to have failed to expand the notion of religious liberty in this manner would have meant maintaining the privilege of religion over nonreligion, thus violating the Establishment Clause. There are, however, other profound implications for the Establishment Clause resulting from this new understanding of the legal status of conscience, and we turn to them in chapter 4.

4

CONSCIENCE AND
THE ESTABLISHMENT CLAUSE

In chapter 3 I advanced the dual notion that (1) what the Free Exercise Clause protects is increasingly understood to refer not just to religion in the traditional sense but to conscience and (2) this enlarged understanding of free exercise was compelled once the courts rejected the belief–action distinction, thus requiring the law to differentiate actions that are secularly motivated from actions reflecting true conviction, whether articulated in religious language or not. Once it is recognized, however, that it is "conscience" that is protected—and not just "religion"—a rather startling implication becomes apparent: If conscience is what can be freely exercised, is it therefore also conscience that Congress must not establish? If so, just what does that mean? We explore these questions in chapter 4.

Nonpreferentialism Exposed

It seems reasonable to expect that the greatest support for the free exercise of religion would come from persons who assign the greatest importance to religion. In one sense that is true, as exemplified in the very broad range of religious leaders included in the support given to the Rev. Sun Myung Moon in his tax evasion case. Carlton Sherwood has listed them (1991:377–78):

> A stranger group of bedfellows would be hard to imagine: the Reverend Jerry Falwell, former Senator Eugene McCarthy, the late Clare Booth Luce, Harvard law professor Laurence Tribe, and Senator Orrin Hatch.

. . . [A] single thread also ties together the liberal American Civil Liberties Union and the Southern Christian Leadership Conference with the conservative Freemen Institute. The same thread connects Baptists and Presbyterians, the Roman Catholic Church and the National Council of Churches, not to mention the avowedly Marxist Spartacist League as well as the states of Hawaii, Oregon, and Rhode Island. Between 1982 and 1984 all of the above and more than thirty other individuals and organizations entered *amicus curiae* . . . briefs [on Moon's behalf].

Moon lost his case despite this outpouring of support, but the reason for the concern is simple to understand. All the sponsors of those briefs could see that if the Internal Revenue Service could punish the founder and leader of the Unification Church on the grounds charged, it could similarly punish them; in the case of religious leaders, it was their own free exercise of religion that was in jeopardy. In any avowedly pluralistic society, then, each religion is likely to recognize that *its* welfare depends upon upholding the free exercise of *all* religions.

We saw in the closing pages of chapter 3, however, that at least some people of religious conviction decry the circumstances whereby "conscience" becomes entitled to the constitutional protection heretofore extended only to "religion." For Richard John Neuhaus, this means that courts look not at the content of belief but at the sincerity with which belief is held. "Individual conviction," he says, has replaced "communal values" (1984:80).

I disagree. When individual conviction or conscience is regarded as religion's legal equivalent, religion as a "communal value" does not disappear, as Neuhaus seems to suggest. Rather, upon close inspection it turns out that communal religion (the "church" or other organized religious activity) merely has to give up a governmental preference it once enjoyed, a recognition now seen to be unconstitutional. The more sensitive the state becomes in protecting conscience, in other words, the more likely it is to uncover heretofore unacknowledged "established" religion, which is then found to be in violation of the Establishment Clause. People who regret this jurisprudential development are often called "nonpreferentialists" because, while they agree that government cannot prefer one religion over another, they do believe government can and should prefer religion over irreligion.

The issue is clearly exhibited in the *Torcaso* case discussed in chapter 3. The Supreme Court in that case, using language it had used before, ruled that government may not force a person "to profess a belief or disbelief in any religion" and thus declared unconstitutional Maryland's constitutional provision requiring a belief in God by anyone serving any public office. On the grounds, then, that Torcaso was free to disbelieve in God and still be a commissioned notary public, the state was compelled to "disestablish" a religious criterion (theistic belief) for taking office. Thus, following his lament that, when conscience became a synonym for religion, "communal values" were replaced by "individual conviction," Neuhaus goes on to say that religion "is no longer a public reality and therefore cannot interfere with public business" (1984:80). This fact Neuhaus laments, but he misperceives the meaning of *Torcaso:* It is not that religion is no longer a public reality but rather that public reality includes a broader conception of religion.

It is not surprising that, when Free Exercise Doctrine extends far enough to recognize consciences not articulated religiously, some people are vexed—not so much because conscientious persons receive benefits as because traditional forms of religion are seen to lose benefits. This, of course, is not the wording used by those who are vexed. They would say, rather, that government is no longer accommodating traditional forms of religion. It is renewed accommodation of *their* religion that they desire, not the newly discovered accommodation of heretofore unprotected consciences. Marvin Frankel makes this point with hyperbole. Labeling as "access seekers" persons who want the wall of separation returned to a lower height, Frankel claims that "the concrete goals of the access seekers reflect mainly crabbed demands for status, authority, and petty but maddening superordination" (1992:639).

Frankel's criticism may be harsh, but it does point up the inherent tension between the Free Exercise Clause and its No Establishment counterpart, or— as some have put it—between the accommodation of religion that the Free Exercise Clause *requires* and the accommodation of religion that the No Establishment Clause *permits.* Persons who support an interpretation of free exercise broad enough to extend to "conscience" seem likely to support an interpretation of No Establishment that finds unconstitutional many religious actions that have previously been accommodated. Put another way, when the rights of free exercise are extended to conscience or conviction, whether articulated religiously or not, heretofore religious actions that have been shown preference because they are *religious* are vulnerable to the charge that they represent an unconstitutional establishment of religion. The conscientious objection cases illustrate this point exactly: If conviction alone, and not identification with a *particular* kind of religious belief, is sufficient to claim CO status, it means that persons holding those particular beliefs were earlier enjoying an unconstitutional special privilege.

Free Exercise
vs. No Establishment

The inherent tension between the two clauses is illustrated in an unusually vivid way in a 1989 Supreme Court case, *County of Allegheny et al. v. American Civil Liberties Union et al.* At issue was the constitutionality of (1) a crèche scene installed in the lobby of Pittsburgh's City-County Building and (2) a Hanukkah menorah placed just outside a nearby building, next to a Christmas tree and a sign saluting liberty. The Court, with four dissenting votes, ruled to outlaw the crèche scene as clearly sending a message of governmental "endorsement" of an obviously Christian symbol, but it ruled in favor of the menorah on the grounds that the menorah, like the Christmas tree, has secular as well as religious connotations and thus could be interpreted as merely a symbol of the winter holiday season.

Ostensibly, these decisions were based on differing interpretations of the Establishment Clause, but the majority opinion—written by Justice Blackmun—and the dissenting opinion—written by Justice Kennedy—make clear that free-exercise considerations lay just beneath the surface of the debate. It is my point here that, because of the inherent tension between the two clauses, establishment-based decisions are likely to involve free-exercise issues as well. The so-called nonpreferentialists—those seeking greater accommodation for religion—do not appreciate this inherent relationship, as we shall now see.

Because the Justices arrive at their opinions after circulating drafts of one another's tentative views of a case, it is not uncommon, in cases having dissenting minorities, for the final majority and minority opinions to include counterarguments as well as arguments. The Allegheny crèche case provides us with an especially vigorous, not to say vituperative, illustration.

After Blackmun introduces the facts of the crèche and the menorah, he first develops the line of reasoning he and other members of the majority have employed in arriving at their opinion.

> This Nation is heir to a history and tradition of religious diversity that dates from the settlement of the North American continent. Sectarian differences among various Christian denominations were central to the origins of our Republic. Since then, adherents of religions too numerous to name have made the United States their home, as have those whose beliefs expressly exclude religion. Precisely because of the religious diversity . . . the Founders added . . . a Bill of Rights, the very first words of which declare: "Congress shall make no law respecting an establishment of religion, or prohibiting the free exercise thereof." Perhaps in the early days of the Republic these words were understood to protect only the diversity within Christianity, but today they are recognized as guaranteeing religious liberty and equality to the infidel, the atheist, or the adherent of a non-Christian faith such as Islam or Judaism. . . . It is settled law that no government official in this Nation may violate these fundamental constitutional rights regarding matters of conscience.

This sets the stage by giving great weight to religious pluralism and the need to safeguard everyone's religious free exercise.

Justice Blackmun then goes on to a lengthy discussion of how the crèche scene violates the No Establishment Clause because it so obviously suggests governmental endorsement of Christianity. But it is just as clear that he also regards such an endorsement as violating the Free Exercise Clause, because it communicates to non-Christians that their religions are *not* endorsed.

Justice Kennedy, joined by Chief Justice Rehnquist and Justices White and Scalia, offers several counterarguments, but the one of interest here is the claim that, in failing to accommodate the crèche scene in a government building, the majority opinion misinterprets the No Establishment Clause:

> Rather than requiring government to avoid any action that acknowledges or aids religion, the Establishment Clause permits government some latitude in recognizing and accommodating the central role religion plays in our society. . . . Any approach less sensitive to our heritage would border on latent hostility toward religion, as it would require government in all its multifaceted roles to acknowledge only the secular, to the exclusion and so to the detriment of the religious. [The consequence is:] Those religions enjoying the largest following must be consigned to the status of least-favored faiths so as to avoid any possible risk of offending members of minority religions.

Blackmun rises to this bait and in so doing reveals how deeply embedded in Free Exercise issues is this No Establishment case:

> Although Justice Kennedy repeatedly accuses the Court of harboring a "latent hostility" . . . toward religion . . . nothing could be further from the truth, and the accusations could be said to be as offensive as they are absurd. Justice Kennedy apparently has misperceived a respect for religious pluralism, a respect commanded by the Constitution, as hostility or indifference to religion. No misperception could be more antithetical to the values embodied in the Establishment Clause. . . . In his attempt to legitimize the display of the crèche . . . Justice Kennedy repeatedly characterizes it as "accommodation" of religion. But accommodation of religion, in order to be permitted under the Establishment Clause, must lift an identifiable burden *on the exercise of religion*. . . . One may agree with Justice Kennedy that the scope of accommodations permissible under the Establishment Clause is larger than the scope of accommodations mandated by the Free Exercise Clause. . . . But a category of "permissible accommodations of religion not required by the Free Exercise Clause" aids the crèche . . . not at all. Prohibiting the display of a crèche at this location . . . does not impose a burden on the practice of Christianity (except to the extent some Christian sect seeks to be an officially

approved religion), and therefore permitting the display is not an "accommodation" of religion in the conventional sense.

In his own words, Justice Blackmun is accusing Justice Kennedy of defending nonpreferentialism, or what Marvin Frankel called "crabbed demands for status, authority, and petty but maddening superordination."

Three years after the *Allegheny* crèche decision a similar issue came before the Supreme Court, and once again nonpreferentialism was debated—separationists vs. accommodationists. What was being challenged in *Lee v. Weisman* (1992) was the practice in a Providence, Rhode Island, junior high school of the principal in inviting local clergy to offer prayer at graduation ceremonies.

Splitting pretty much as they had in *Allegheny,* the Justices declared 5–4 that such prayers are unconstitutional. This time the dissent was written by Justice Scalia, who reiterated the nonpreferentialist credo that "government policies of accommodation, acknowledgment, and support for religion are an accepted part of our political and cultural heritage." We saw at the end of chapter 2 that Scalia's dissent in this case has been nominated as the "highwater mark" for its "impatient distaste for deviant sensibilities getting in the way of majority preferences" (Frankel 1994:12), and it is exactly that impatient distaste that raised the ire of Justice Souter to the point of writing a rebuttal as a majority concurring opinion in *Lee v. Weisman.* Souter's claim:

> Since *Everson,* we have consistently held the [Establishment] Clause applicable no less to governmental acts favoring religion generally than to acts favoring one religion over others. Thus in *Engel v. Vitale* . . . (1962), we held that the public schools may not subject their students to readings of any prayer, however "denominationally neutral." . . . More recently, in *Wallace v. Jaffree* . . . (1985), we held that an Alabama moment-of-silence statute passed for the sole purpose of "returning voluntary prayer to public schools" . . . violated the Establishment Clause even though it did not encourage students to pray to any particular deity. We said that "when the underlying principle has been examined in the crucible of litigation, the Court has unambiguously concluded that the individual freedom of conscience protected by the First Amendment embraces the right to select any religious faith or none at all."

It seems that what strict separationists see clearly—that once conscience is accorded the same protection that religion receives, Establishment Clause cases necessarily involve free-exercise considerations—accommodationists do not see. David A. J. Richards goes so far as to claim that this relationship was known, at least to some, from the very beginning of the Republic. Thomas Jefferson, he says (1986:12),

> elaborates the underlying moral ideal of respect for conscience to indulge not only free exercise, but any form of religious qualification for civil rights or any compulsion of tax money for support of religious beliefs, even one's own. Since Jefferson believes that the rights of conscience are inalienable rights . . . he regards any state financial or other support for the propagation of religious belief as tyranny.

Actually, according to James Washington (1992:21–22), while most of Jefferson's colleagues would have agreed that the "rights of conscience" are natural and inalienable, "this did not forestall nearly 150 years of theological and philosophical debates about the meaning of this phrase." While the debates go on, therefore, and the role of conscience is by no means fixed in law, Mark DeWolfe Howe's "radical principle of liberty" does seem to be emerging as the free-exercise implications found in Establishment cases are recognized. Granted, it has taken a long time to understand that when, say, a crèche scene is supported by public tax money it is not just non-Christian believers whose truly free exercise of religion is being limited; also limited is the truly free exercise of Christian believers who observe their government dictating—however gently—*how* their Christianity is to be conceived and practiced. And that, as Jefferson would say, is "tyranny."

Freedom of Conscience and the Establishment Clause

To this point, we have been looking at cases in which unconstitutional state endorsement has been bestowed on practices that are obviously religious—a crèche in a county building, prayer at a public school commencement—and I have argued that just as these are clearly Establishment cases, so are they clearly Free Exercise cases also, inasmuch as they represent government-mandated practices that deny conscientious discretion to persons entitled to such conscientious discretion. This is the line of reasoning by which the Supreme Court rejected a 1928 Arkansas law prohibiting the teaching of evolution in any public school in the state (*Epperson v. Arkansas,* 1967). Justice Fortas, who wrote the unanimous opinion, perceived the law's purpose as preventing teachers from discussing evolution "because it is contrary to the belief of some that the Book of Genesis must be the exclusive source of doctrine as to the origin of man." But such a law, he said, conflicts with the Free Exercise Clause and not just the No Establishment Clause. Indeed, in an analysis of Fortas's opinion, Kyron Huigens, in a law review article significantly entitled "Science, Freedom of Conscience, and the Establishment Clause," says that Fortas was suggesting "that orthodoxy, indoctrination, and conformity—in themselves, and not merely as features of an established church—are effects of government action which it is the function of the establishment clause to prevent" (1989:89).

This principle—that violations of the No Establishment Clause may violate the Free Exercise Clause by infringing on conscience—can also be seen in the 1984 *Grand Rapids School District v. Ball,* where publicly paid teachers were no longer allowed to teach secular subjects in parochial schools. In the majority opinion, Justice Brennan noted that if any religious indoctrination were to occur it "would have devastating effects on the right of each individual voluntarily to determine what to believe (and what not to believe) free of any coercive pressure from the state." (This decision was modified in 1997 in *Agostini v. Felton* to allow publicly funded special education teachers to teach inside parochial schools.)

Free Exercise implications that arise in Establishment cases are relatively easy to discern, once conscience is seen as the legal equivalent of religion. Such implications are less obvious in other kinds of cases, however, especially cases that ostensibly lie outside the realm of church and state, as do my next three examples. Constitutionally, these cases were decided not on First Amendment grounds but on the Due Process Clause of the Fourteenth Amendment. Ostensibly, then, they deal with "liberty," not "religion," but it will be seen that conscience plays a constant role in these cases. Significantly, all three examples are found on the battleground of what James D. Hunter calls America's "culture wars" (1991). That is to say, they are among the issues that currently exercise American citizens greatly, suggesting that though they may not generally be perceived as church-state issues, they nonetheless are debates about the "soul" of America. I refer to abortion, euthanasia, and homosexuality.

Abortion

In 1979, the U.S. Supreme Court, by a vote of 5–4 in *Harris v. McRae,* upheld the constitutionality of the congressional legislation known as the Hyde Amendment, which prohibits federal funding for Medicaid abortions. Cora McRae, a pregnant indigent woman eligible for Medicaid, desired an abortion for therapeutic reasons but was turned down. She brought suit on several grounds: that she was denied due process and that both the Establishment Clause and the Free Exercise Clause were violated in her case. The majority rejected all three of these claims. McRae's due process was not violated, the majority said, because she was not denied abortion, only the federal funds to pay for it. The claim based on the Establishment Clause was rejected because, while some religions do regard abortion as sinful, that fact does not prevent government from passing laws outlawing abortion. Finally, McRae's Free Exercise argument was rejected because she did not allege, let alone prove, that she sought an abortion "under compulsion of religious belief." We will see that the four dissenters in this case have a markedly different picture of the issue.

It is not farfetched to suggest that, contrary to the majority view, McRae's free exercise of religion *was* violated, at least if "conscience" is what it is that can be freely exercised. A hint of this perspective is found in the dissents of Justices Stevens and Brennan. Both accept the view that McRae was being treated unfairly because she was poor, and, as Stevens writes,

the government must use neutral criteria in distributing benefits. . . . [I]t may not create exceptions for the sole purpose of furthering a governmental interest that is constitutionally subordinate to the individual interest that the entire program was designed to protect.

And what is the individual interest in this case? It is the provision of health care to indigent citizens. Once such a provision is in place, the dissenters agree, the state may not use its financial power to influence a woman's freedom to choose whether to have an abortion. That freedom, needless to say, is constitutionally guaranteed by *Roe v. Wade* (1973), which found a woman's absolute right to abortion in the first trimester of her pregnancy. Justice Brennan goes further in his dissent, however:

> My focus . . . is upon the coercive impact of the congressional decision to fund one outcome of pregnancy—childbirth—while not funding the other—abortion. . . . [T]he Hyde Amendment is a transparent attempt by the Legislative Branch to impose the political majority's judgment of the morally acceptable and socially desirable preference on a sensitive and intimate decision that the Constitution entrusts to the individual.

Might Brennan have been comfortable tacking on the word "conscience" to that last sentence? As I said in the Introduction, this is not a legal analysis in the usual sense but rather an effort to extract a cultural interpretation using legal cases. Obviously, therefore, I do not know how Justice Brennan would respond to my hypothetical question, but the hint to which I referred a few paragraphs back is found further on in Brennan's dissent when he draws a parallel between McRae and Seventh-Day Adventist Sherbert, who was denied unemployment compensation by the state when she resigned her job rather than work on Saturdays. The Supreme Court then reversed. Brennan quotes from the majority opinion that he himself wrote in that case (*Sherbert v. Verner,* 1963):

> The ruling [denying her benefits] forces her to choose between following the precepts of her religion and forfeiting benefits, on the one hand, and abandoning one of the precepts of her religion in order to accept work, on the other hand. Governmental imposition of such a choice puts the same kind of burden upon the free exercise of religion as would a fine imposed against appellant for her Saturday worship.

I am *not* suggesting that McRae's free exercise of her religion (in the narrow sense) was assaulted by the Hyde Amendment; I *am* suggesting that the Hyde Amendment represents an unconstitutional establishment of one conscientious position over alternative conscientious positions—which violates McRae's freedom of conscience and thus the Free Exercise Clause as interpreted here.

This interpretation is more clearly illustrated in another abortion case nine years later, *Webster v. Reproductive Health Services.* The same four justices dissented, but it is Justice Stevens's dissent we attend to here. *Webster* resulted from a certain Missouri legislative bill, the preamble of which declared that the life of "each human being begins at conception." Three other provisions stipulated certain regulations to be followed in abortion cases: that no public funds be used to encourage abortion, that no public employees or facilities be used in performing abortions, and that a viability test be performed on the fetus of any woman seeking abortion if reason exists to believe she is twenty or more weeks pregnant.

Justice Stevens is bothered chiefly by the preamble. He writes:

> I am persuaded that the absence of any secular purpose for the legislative declarations that life begins at conception and that conception occurs at fertilization makes the relevant portion of the preamble invalid under the Establishment Clause. . . . This conclusion does not, and could not, rest on the fact that the statement happens to coincide with the tenets of certain religions . . . or on the fact that the legislators who voted to enact it may have been motivated by religious considerations. . . . Rather, it rests on the fact that the preamble, an unequivocal endorsement of a religious tenet of some but by no means all Christian faiths, serves no identifiable secular purpose. That fact alone compels a conclusion that the statute violates the Establishment Clause.

It is important to note that Justice Stevens is not choosing secularism over religion. He is not stating that life does *not* begin at conception. Rather, he is saying that whether or not life begins at conception is necessarily a conscience issue, not because religions have views on this issue but because no secular purpose has been identified. The implication is that even if the pro-choice supporters in this case did not regard their position as "religious," that position was conscientiously held and therefore, in Justice

Stevens's view, entitled to the same First Amendment protection enjoyed by their opponents—the right to "select any religious faith or none at all." Put another way, Justice Stevens recognizes that the question of when life begins involves at least two conflicting positions, each entitled to be freely exercised and neither entitled to be "established" in law.

As I have said, I am using examples—that of abortion thus far—to illustrate a more general perspective on conscience and thus religious liberty. It is time now to address this general perspective.

Is it possible, we can ask, to believe profoundly that abortion is evil and still leave the decision to abort to the pregnant woman whose life and conscience is most directly connected to the choice? That pair of views, writes Ronald Dworkin (1993:15), "is not only consistent but is in keeping with a great tradition of freedom of conscience in modern pluralistic democracies." What is really at issue in abortion cases, Dworkin insists (1993:25–26), is

> whether state legislatures have the constitutional power to decide which intrinsic values all citizens must respect, and how, and whether legislatures may prohibit abortion on that ground. . . . *[F]reedom of choice about abortion is a necessary implication of the religious freedom guaranteed by the First Amendment* [emphasis added].

Peter Wenz makes the same argument in his book *Abortion Rights as Religious Freedom.*

David A. J. Richards makes the case more generally. The moral basis of the Free Exercise Clause, he writes, is "immunizing from state coercion the exercise of conceptions of life well and ethically lived and expressive of a mature person's rational and reasonable powers." Likewise, the No Establishment Clause prohibits the state from interfering with the "forming and changing of those conceptions" (1986:140).

Euthanasia

Less space is needed for the euthanasia illustration because, as has often been noted, the legal and moral issues are much the same as those in the case of abortion. Both involve competing interests that must be weighed and a balance found. Moreover, in both instances these interests change through time, which alters the balance and thus also alters the state's interest in intervening. As a Ninth Circuit Federal Court decision regarding assisted suicide recently stated, "[B]oth types of case raise issues of life and death, and both arouse similar religious and moral concerns. Both also present basic questions about an individual's right of choice" (*Compassion in Dying v. State of Washington,* 1996).

As in the case of abortion, the significant issue is this: On what basis may the state restrict an individual's right of choice? The first case we will examine (*Cruzan v. Director, Missouri Department of Health,* 1990) involved a Missouri law that required "clear and convincing evidence" of an incompetent, terminally ill person's wish to have life-sustaining treatment withdrawn before any such withdrawal could be approved. Nancy Cruzan was a victim of an auto accident that had left her for six years in a "permanent vegetative state." The testimony of her parents and her one-time housemate, that Nancy often expressed her desire to avoid being kept alive by such means, was found insufficient by a lower court, and a five-person majority of the Supreme Court could find no constitutional basis for finding otherwise. As in other cases we are examining here, however, the cultural meaning I am identifying is found not in the majority opinion but in the dissent. It is, of course, no coincidence that the dissenters in this case are the four whose views we have already encountered—Brennan, Blackmun, Marshall, and Stevens. In *Cruzan* it is Stevens's dissent that best illustrates my argument:

> Missouri's regulation is an unreasonable intrusion upon traditionally private matters encompassed within the liberty protected by the Due Process Clause. . . . [N]ot much may be said with confidence about death unless it is said from faith, and that alone is reason enough to protect the freedom to conform choices about death to individual conscience. . . . Missouri asserts that its policy is related to a state interest in the protection of life. In my view, however, it is an effort to define life, rather than to protect it, that is the heart of Missouri's policy. Missouri insists, without regard to Nancy Cruzan's own interests, upon equaling her life with

the biological persistence of her bodily functions. . . . [T]here is a serious question as to whether the mere persistence of their bodies is "life" as that word is commonly understood, or as it is used in both the Constitution and the Declaration of Independence. . . . It is not within the province of secular government to circumscribe the liberties of the people by regulations designed wholly for the purpose of *establishing a sectarian definition of life* [emphasis added].

It is hardly surprising that in this dissent Justice Stevens footnotes his earlier dissent in the *Webster* abortion case. In both cases, he sees legislation that arbitrarily defines life—when it begins in *Webster,* when it ends in *Cruzan*—the effect each time being the unnecessary and unconstitutional establishment of an ultimate perspective not shared by all. If not an establishment of religion in the narrow sense, it *is* an establishment of one conscientious position, disregarding—even outlawing—alternative conscientious positions. That is what Justice Stevens objects to.

In 1996 the Ninth Circuit Court of Appeals declared unconstitutional the Washington State law making a felony of any physician-assisted suicide (*Compassion in Dying v. State of Washington*). The vote was 8–3, which, along with the fact that this appellate case challenges the *Cruzan* decision, probably destined it to go to the U.S. Supreme Court. Indeed, in October 1996 the Court agreed to hear the appeal, joining the Ninth Circuit decision to a similar decision arising in the Second Circuit. Oral arguments were heard in January 1997, and the following June the Court overturned both circuit courts' decisions (*Washington et al. v. Glucksberg et al.* and *Vacco et al. v. Quill et al.*).

Many legal experts, perhaps most, predicted that the Supreme Court would reverse the two decisions upholding assisted suicides. Justice Scalia, at least, was on record from a speech to a Virginia college audience in the spring of 1996 as doubting whether the question of assisted suicide should even be decided by the Supreme Court. "Why," he was quoted as saying, "would you leave that to nine lawyers, for heaven's sake?"

Because I am not undertaking a legal analysis here, how the Supreme Court decided the assisted suicide issue is not my direct concern. My concern rather is to expose the religious liberty theme, the "conscience" theme, that runs through legal disputes even when they are not ostensibly church-state cases. The Washington State case serves this purpose well.

The terminally ill patients who joined their doctors as plaintiffs were in this instance judged competent to make a decision to withhold life-support assistance for themselves. They could, for example, have refused medication that extended their lives. What they could *not* do is expect their doctors to assist them in accomplishing a sure and painless end to life. (The Second Circuit case hinged on exactly this point; the judges found discrimination in the inability of persons *not* on life-support assistance to hasten their death, which people who reject such assistance *are* able to do.) The majority of the Ninth Circuit judges who heard this case decided that this restriction on physicians is unconstitutional, using not a First Amendment basis in their decision but a Fourteenth (Due Process) Amendment basis.

The difference in the basis on which the decision rests is important. First Amendment rights are "fundamental" or "inalienable," and only a state's "compelling interest" can justify their restriction. The rights guaranteed by the Due Process Clause, often called "liberty interests," though not less important than First Amendment rights, can be thwarted more easily because, not being "fundamental," they are balanced against governmental interests that might easily outweigh them. Thus, had the patient in *Cruzan* been competent to ask that she be taken off life support, her "liberty interest" would have trumped the state's interest in preserving life. Because Nancy Cruzan was incompetent, however, the state's interest in requiring "clear and convincing evidence" of her wishes in this matter outweighed whatever "liberty interest" she had—at least that is how the majority decided.

The Ninth Circuit was mindful of the seriousness of the case before them. A lower court had found for the plaintiffs in 1994. Upon a first appeal to the Ninth Circuit, that judgment was reversed two to one, which led to an eleven-judge panel that reheard the case and affirmed the lower court's ruling. After laying out the circumstances of the case, the majority strikes the seriousness note:

There is no litmus test for courts to apply when deciding whether or not a liberty interest exists under the Due Process Clause. Our decisions involve difficult judgments regarding the conscience, traditions, and fundamental tenets of our nation. We must sometimes apply those basic principles in light of changing values based on shared experience. Other times we must apply them to new problems arising out of the development and use of new technologies. In all cases, our analysis of the applicability of the protections of the Constitution must be made in light of existing circumstances as well as our historic traditions.

The Ninth Circuit Court then reviewed a great many cases from the past in which "personal" matters have been adjudicated, deciding that "few decisions are more personal, intimate or important than the decision to end one's life, especially when the reason for doing so is to avoid excessive and protracted pain." It then quotes from a 1992 Supreme Court decision (*Planned Parenthood v. Casey*) that

> the most intimate and personal choices a person may make in a lifetime, choices central to personal dignity and autonomy, are central to the liberty protected by the Fourteenth Amendment. At the heart of liberty is the right to define one's own concept of existence, of meaning, of the universe, and of the mystery of human life. Beliefs about these matters could not define the attributes of personhood were they formed under compulsion of the State.

On this basis, then, the Ninth Circuit Court in this assisted suicide case wrote the summary statement so widely quoted in news stories about this case:

> A competent terminally ill adult, having lived nearly the full measure of his life, has a strong liberty interest in choosing a dignified and humane death rather than being reduced at the end of his existence to a childlike state of helplessness, diapered, sedated, incontinent.

That summary statement does not highlight the relevance this case has for my purposes, however. What does this is the decision's concluding paragraph:

There is one final point we must emphasize. Some argue strongly that decisions regarding matters affecting life or death should not be made by the courts. Essentially, we agree with that proposition. In this case, by permitting the individual to exercise the right to choose we are following the constitutional mandate to take such decisions out of the hands of the government, both state and federal, and to put them where they rightly belong, in the hands of the people. We are allowing individuals to make the decisions that so profoundly affect their very existence — and precluding the state from intruding excessively into that critical realm. . . . Those who believe strongly that death must come without physician assistance are free to follow that creed, be they doctors or patients. *They are not free, however, to force their views, their religious convictions, or their philosophies on all the other members of a democratic society, and to compel those whose values differ with theirs to die painful, protracted, and agonizing deaths* [emphasis added].

The moral issues involved in euthanasia thus transcend the question of life versus death. They include choice and dignity and self-direction. They ask of us not whether life is sacred but how the sanctity of life is to be understood (see Dworkin 1993: chap. 7; Urofsky 1993). One might expect a more secure majority opinion in this case were it decided on First Amendment grounds. Contrary to Justice Scalia's view, that this is a legislative, not a judicial, matter, this issue is exactly one that, in the words of Justice Jackson quoted in chapter 3, should "not be submitted to vote" or "depend on the outcome" of elections.

As I have indicated, the reasoning of the Ninth Circuit Court was rejected — unanimously — by the Supreme Court. Chief Justice Rehnquist wrote the opinion, joined by four other Justices. The remaining four, while concurring in the outcome, arrived at that outcome by an alternate path. First, they note that laws now permit physicians to prescribe drugs for patients sufficient to control pain, despite the risk that those drugs themselves will kill. Second, however, in rejecting the claims made by the states of Washington and New York, these four Justices recognize that there are grounds for finding "a right to die with dignity" (Justice Breyer, concurring opinion in the two cases). Justice Stevens is even more outspoken:

> A State, like Washington, that has authorized the death penalty and thereby has concluded that the sanctity of human life does not require that it always be preserved, must acknowledge that there are situations in which an interest in hastening death is legitimate. Indeed, not only is that interest sometimes legitimate, I am also convinced that there are times when it is entitled to constitutional protection.

The "liberty interest" Justice Stevens identified in *Cruzan* remains real for him at least. In the meantime, these two cases have upheld the right of states to outlaw assisted suicide; what they don't do is prohibit states from changing their laws to permit assisted suicide—in accordance with what polls show the public desires by a margin of five to four. Certainly the cases that arose in Washington and New York are not the end of this issue. If my analysis here is correct, the eventual outcome is predictable.

Homosexuality

It has been suggested that the euthanasia issue is now about where the abortion issue was twenty years ago. Dispute continues over abortion, however, even if the principle of a constitutional right to privacy appears to be reasonably secure. That suggests that euthanasia will likewise be debated for years to come. Even newer on the legal front is the issue of homosexuality, an issue having much in common with abortion and euthanasia, at least to those who follow my reasoning here.

One feature the three issues share is a certain divide. In each instance there are those on one side who find a certain action objectionable, even evil. And in each instance there are those on the opposing side who find the same action desirable, even noble. A major difference between the two sides is that the first side has not only had its viewpoint recognized as the dominant cultural viewpoint but has also seen it written into law. This has left members of the second side subject to criminal prosecution as well as social denunciation.

A second feature the three issues share is this: While the one side articulates its viewpoint in religious language, the second side articulates its viewpoint in the language of conscience that often omits reference to religion. This appears to give a public relations advantage to the first side. Does it also give it a constitutional advantage? I would argue that it does not and should not. I would argue further that the second side can show that its opponents enjoy a two-fold unconstitutional privilege: (1) an unconstitutional "establishment" of the first side's viewpoint and (2) an unconstitutional "violation" of the second side's right to the free exercise of conscience.

Only recently has homosexuality joined this company of issues. The Georgia sodomy case (*Bowers v. Hardwick,* 1985) was technically not a decision about same-sex activity, since heterosexual sodomy was also outlawed by the Georgia statute, but it nonetheless stands as a measure of Supreme Court thinking only a decade ago. The majority voted to uphold the Georgia statute, while the dissenters saw that Georgia was imposing a particular viewpoint that by no means was shared by all. Indeed, Justice Lewis Powell, who voted with the majority, is reported to have said, after he retired, that he had concluded that he voted wrongly. The legal standing of homosexuality is obviously "ripening" as gay and lesbian persons are insisting on their rights as citizens, including the right to marry. As with abortion and euthanasia, these demands touch on the very core of what "conscience" means.

In his book *The Case for Same-Sex Marriage,* William N. Eskridge, Jr., makes the legal argument on the basis of two claims (1996:123). Existing state policies, he says, "discriminate unlawfully when, without substantial justification, they pick and choose the citizens granted the fundamental right to marry." Those same policies, he goes on, also discriminate unlawfully when "they exclude citizens from any right merely because of their sex or sexual orientation."

As with the argument for legal abortion and legal euthanasia, Eskridge rests his claims for same-sex marriage on the equal protection clause of the U.S. Constitution's Fourteenth Amendment; this is a "liberty" right, not a "free exercise of religion" right he is discussing. As I have contended right along, however, in the absence of a compelling state interest and/or secular purpose, homosexual rights, like abortion rights and euthanasia rights, reflect the rights of conscience.

Andrew Sullivan has made the case for this last assertion in his carefully reasoned *Virtually Normal,* an analysis of several stances toward homosexuality to be found in contemporary America. Sullivan says that

the vast majority of people engaging in homosexual acts regard those acts as an extension of their deepest emotional and sexual desires, desires which they do not believe they have chosen and which they cannot believe are always and everywhere wrong [1995:30]. . . . When the subject of homosexuality emerges, it is always subject to emotive passion, and affects matters of religious conscience [1995:158]. . . . The act of openly conceding one's homosexuality is in some ways an act of faith, of faith in the sturdiness of one's own identity and the sincerity of one's own heart [1995:166]. . . . Marriage is not simply a private contract; it is a social and public recognition of a private commitment. As such, it is the highest public recognition of personal integrity [1995:179].

Near the end of his book, Sullivan admits that homosexuality is not the equivalent of a "religious calling," but who can doubt that—to him certainly, but obviously to many others as well—it involves the very core of one's being. It involves conscience.

Conclusion

In this chapter on the No Establishment Clause, I have had much to say about Free Exercise. It has been my goal here to show the inevitable linkage of these two clauses. That can be done directly in cases where "establishment" clearly involves what all would regard as religion, such as a crèche on public land or a prayer at a public school commencement. Once Free Exercise is conceived to be the free exercise of conscience, however, even cases falling outside the church-state realm may reveal the implications of the linkage between the two Religion Clauses. It happens that the illustrations discussed in this chapter rest on the Due Process clause; they involve claims that one's liberty is being denied unconstitutionally. But in each of those illustrations—abortion, euthanasia, and homosexuality—we could observe that laws enacted to establish what may be the majority viewpoint can do harm to the minority conscience. This, I have argued, violates both Religion Clauses, in spirit if not in some narrow legal sense. As David Richards says, "The antiestablishment worry is not over regulations of conscience in general, but over sectarian conscience using state power to unfair . . . advantage inconsistent with equal respect for conscience" (1986:145).

Richards's statement suggests my next step: If only *some* regulations of conscience violate the Constitution and other regulations do not, how do we tell the difference? That is the topic of chapter 5.

5

JUDGING CLAIMS
OF CONSCIENCE

I have already indicated that my sympathies lie with the separationists on the sorts of issues I have been discussing. That means I incline toward expanding religious liberty to the point of recognizing conscience as the equivalent of religion. Moreover, I would invoke "the radical principle of liberty" not just in cases resting on the Religion Clauses of the First Amendment but also in cases that rest on the Due Process Clause and thus may involve profound questions of conscience. This is because life, liberty, and the right to own property—which the Due Process Clause guarantees—often involve such issues as personal identity and human dignity. While these issues are not necessarily articulated in religious language, they do touch on conscience, which—as I argued in chapter 3—logically precedes religion. That is to say, the American conception of religious liberty—the conception that *gives rise* to notions of Free Exercise and No Establishment—*presupposes* an inalienable right to conscience. Put yet another way, by placing certain restraints on the role of religion in the public square, these conceptually prior claims of conscience are more likely to be recognized.

I do not pretend that this perspective, and the judicial decisions this perspective would yield, are now accepted views. In my scheme, some abortion rights would be beyond retraction, assisted suicide of the sort discussed in chapter 4 would be constitutional, and homosexual marriage would enjoy the same state recognition now accorded heterosexual marriage. But opposition to each of these outcomes is rampant, and prudence suggests that the political process that eventually will bring them about lags behind the development and acceptance of the socio-philosophical rationale that justifies those outcomes. My argument, it will be recalled from chapter 2 especially, is that the historical shift has been from greater accommodation to less and from less separation to more. The finding that "free exercise" refers to a free conscience, and a correlative finding that therefore laws may establish one conscientious position to the detriment of other conscientious positions, identifies the direction of change being predicted. My claim here concerns that direction itself, not how soon certain positions on a line in that direction will be reached.

Consciences Must Be Judged

To say that conscience is being accorded greater and greater recognition is not to say that all conscience rights are equally valid. Just as, from the beginning of our national government, religious freedom was never understood to be absolute, neither is freedom of conscience absolute. Some claims made in the name of conscience are appropriately denied, and so it will always be; conscience is no more entitled to unbridled expression than is religion.

This issue is quite uncomplicated in those cases arising in the free-exercise arena, where some persons in the name of conscience are claiming the right to *do* what others may *not do*, or the right *not to do* what others *must do*. As with religious free exercise, so with conscientious free exercise: Something along the lines of the *Sherbert* test has to come into play. Is the conscience burdened? Has the state a compelling interest that justifies this burden? Is a less burdensome solution available?

It is when conscience claims extend into the "establishment" arena that line-drawing problems ensue, as was clearly shown in the *Torcaso* case, where an atheist was initially denied a notary public's license by the State of Maryland. Only indirectly was Roy Torcaso's "free exercise" of his atheism being denied. Indeed, in one sense he enjoyed full freedom to exercise his atheism. What was occurring *directly,* however, was the improper "establishment" of theism at the expense of Torcaso's conscience.

It is in this establishment arena where bitter debate can occur between separationists and accommodationists. Allowing nonreligious persons some of the free-exercise rights heretofore reserved for the religious is one thing; withdrawing a privilege that has been reserved for the religious (or for just certain kinds of religious) on the grounds that consciences are being violated is quite another.

Objections to this line of reasoning are readily understood when they come from persons such as Richard John Neuhaus and Stephen Carter, whose religious sensibilities are offended and whose religious privileges are diluted by virtue of being shared with the "non"-religious. The issue of public school religious practices provides an example, after teacher-led prayer and devotional Bible reading were outlawed after 1963. It is apparently difficult for some, perhaps especially those on the Christian Right, to conceive of fellow citizens who are opposed to those practices, who desire not that religion be driven out of public life but that it not enjoy tax-funded sponsorship. It is even more difficult, no doubt, for such people to imagine that state endorsement of *their* religious practices can be an affront to the consciences of other people.

Those who bemoan this recognition of conscience at the seeming expense of their religion often claim that religion has been pushed out of the public realm, and in one sense that is true. But it does not follow that conscience has been pushed out as well. Indeed, it is difficult to name many public issues currently under debate in contemporary America that are *not* entangled in profoundly held convictions, conscientiously argued. The issues of abortion, euthanasia, and homosexuality discussed in chapter 4 are only three examples. Charges, then, that religion has been "pushed" out of the public realm miss a fundamental point, and parallel charges that the result is the establishment of "secular humanism" miss the point even more. The point is that in order to protect and honor everyone's conscience—including the consciences of those who do not articulate their consciences in religious terms—all consciences must be translated into terms that every participant can be expected to recognize.

Why, then, does Richard John Neuhaus maintain that "secularism" insists on pushing religion out of discussions of public matters? Why does Stephen Carter decry a "culture of disbelief" when it comes to important social issues, imagining thereby that religion is being ignored? The answer so far offered here has been a simple one: Those analysts are not prepared to recognize as "religious" any conscientious claims made in language that does not use traditional religion's terms.

Consider this statement by Neuhaus (1984:33):

> Without a transcendent or religious point of reference, conflicts of values cannot be resolved; there can only be procedures for their temporary accommodation. Conflicts over values are viewed not as conflicts between contending truths but as conflicts between contending interests.

Surely this is an incorrect analysis. Any society, whether "secularized" or not, will experience conflict under the conditions Neuhaus describes here. Neither does it matter whether the conflict is between "truths" or "interests." What matters is that two contradictory moral codes appear in a society, and, if the conscientiously held values of both contending parties are to be honored to the point of being recognized, a way must be found to resolve the conflict between them. And should that resolution, in effect, choose one position over the other, the justification must be in terms that the "losing" position understands and can be expected to accept. It is obvious, therefore, that employing the religious language of either of the contending factions is *not* a means of resolution.

One is puzzled, therefore, when Stephen Carter, in discussing the difficulty in conversations between different believers or between believer and nonbeliever, writes, "What is needed is not a requirement that the religiously devout choose a form of dialogue that liberalism accepts, but that liberalism develop a politics that accepts whatever form of dialogue a member of the public offers" (1993:230). But choosing the "form of dialogue" is exactly the rub! Of course the religiously devout are not to be excluded because they are religiously devout, but neither are they exempt from engaging in a form of dialogue acceptable to all. That is what "liberalism" requires—not that religious motivation, language, and reasons be excluded but that they be translated for all to understand. In this context, incidentally, many use not the word "liberalism" but the phrase "secular humanism" and charge that it is illegally the real "established" religion. But as used here, secular humanism is not a system of ideas equivalent to a religion and thus competing with it; it is a language of translation, discussion, and articulation. Of course, should the claim be made that this language is the *only* language reflecting reality, the phrase might better be capitalized as Secular Humanism. In upper-case form it would then be subject to the same constraints all religions face in the legal arena—excluded from endorsement in public schools, for example, but otherwise allowed considerable freedom of expression. Just as students can (and should) be taught that there are Catholics, Jews, Muslims, and so on, so can they be taught that Secular Humanists exist. The language in which all such viewpoints get expressed, however, is the language of lower-case secular humanism.

President Clinton, in the guidelines he issued on July 12, 1995, concerning "Religious Expressions in Public Schools," captures the sense of both the permissible and the impermissible. Regarding "free exercise," the President writes that

> nothing in the First Amendment converts our public schools into religion-free zones, or requires all religious expression to be left behind at the schoolhouse door. While the government may not use schools to coerce the consciences of our students, or to convey official endorsement of religion, the government's schools also may not discriminate against private religious expression during the school day.

As for what is allowed under "establishment," the guidelines say:

> Though schools must be neutral with respect to religion, they may play an active role with respect to teaching civic values and virtues, and the moral code that holds us together as a community. The fact that some of these values are held also by religions does not make it unlawful to teach them in school.

I interpret this statement to mean that teaching (lower-case) secular humanism is not just permitted but also appropriate.

Kathleen Sullivan (1992:197) makes the last point this way:

> [T]he negative bar against establishment of religion implies the affirmative "establishment" of a civil order for the resolution of public moral disputes. . . . Religious teachings as expressed in public debate may in-

fluence the civil public order but public moral disputes may be resolved only on grounds articulable in secular terms.

What separationists thus seem to understand more clearly than accommodationists is that the religiously plural society that honors religious liberty cannot give privileged status to religion on the basis of the nature and content of its beliefs. To do that is necessarily to establish or favor some religion(s) over others. The solution therefore is to define religion not by content but by function, which is the manner by which conscience becomes, for legal purposes, the equivalent of religion. It is also the reason why traditional religion appears to some to have lost its privileged status.

It is clear to separationists, however—to those who favor the "radical principle of religious liberty"—that over and beyond claims of conscience that are entitled to constitutional protection, unless a compelling reason exists to curtail them, there are many other settings in which conscience is—perhaps inadvertently—not given its due. In chapter 4 we looked at three such illustrations where, I claimed, conscience is unjustly burdened: abortion, euthanasia, and homosexuality. Obviously there are other settings where conscience may or may not be unjustly burdened. In such instances, how are we to tell?

When Conscience Is Curtailed

The idea that religious liberty is not absolute when it comes to religious behavior is hardly new. As we saw in chapter 3, the principle entered constitutional law in 1879 in the *Reynolds* case, which found that while government cannot interfere with "mere religious beliefs" it may interfere with a practice such as polygamy. But the idea was well known much before then. A century before, for example, William Livingston of New Haven rephrased what he called a "Puritan principle" to read, "The civil Power hath no jurisdiction over the Sentiments or Opinions of the subject, till such Opinions break out into Actions prejudicial to the Community, and then it is not the Opinion but the Action that is the Object of our Punishment" (Shipton 1965:143). Thomas Jefferson himself called for government to interfere with religion only "when principles break out into overt acts against peace and good order" (*A Bill for Establishing Religious Freedom,* introduced into the Virginia legislature in 1779 and passed in 1786). Common sense, of course, suggests that any group arriving at a point where freedom of belief is an ideal to be sought will quickly realize that behavioral license cannot follow. The interesting question is thus on what basis people's behavior—behavior that is religiously or conscientiously motivated—may be constrained by the state.

The Supreme Court provides some clues to this issue in its range of decisions. Most obvious perhaps is the concept of "compelling interest" that the state must have before limiting persons' right to the free exercise of religion. (Perhaps, after *Boerne v. Flores,* the "compelling interest" concept is not so obvious.) Because that particular right is inalienable in the American scheme, it cannot be taken away but only limited, and then only if the state has a clearly overriding reason to do so. Moreover, not all state interests that some might consider important will qualify as justifiable. For example, Connecticut had a valid reason to keep peace in the community and considered the Jehovah's Witness Cantwell a threat to that peace, but the Court ruled that Cantwell's free-exercise rights trumped Connecticut's interest; the latter was not important enough. In a comparable case, the Court decided that the U.S. Army's need to maintain morale through a uniform dress code was compelling enough to deny an Orthodox Jewish officer the right to wear a yarmulke while on duty.

A variant on the compelling-interest standard is seen in the case of public school prayer and Bible reading, practices that continue in many communities. Where they still occur, local citizens claim that "everybody" wants such practices to continue, which in their minds is everybody's free-exercise right. Experience shows, however, that time and again since 1963, when the issue is heard in courts of law, judges find that school-sponsored prayers at commencements or football games violate the No Establishment Clause; in effect, the law finds a compelling enough reason to constrain those religious practices.

How to Judge the
Claims of Conscience

As a first step in deciding whether claims of conscience may or may not be recognized in the law, courts assess not just the burden placed on conscience but also the seriousness of the state's need to curtail those claims. In principle this first step is not problematic, however complicated it may be empirically to execute.

A second step, however, is more difficult *in principle;* we have already reviewed how, in a number of cases, the difference (or at least *one* difference) between the Supreme Court majority and minority opinions hinges on this issue. It is this: Does the regulation that curtails (or *would* curtail) conscientious claims have a clearly *secular* purpose? Consider the 1993 *Church of the Lukumi Babalu Aye* case, which declared unconstitutional Hialeah's law prohibiting animal sacrifice. Though disagreeing about other aspects of the case, the Justices were unanimous in agreeing that the law not only served no secular purpose—for example, it did not also outlaw the killing of animals in slaughterhouses, or the killing of fish and game caught by individuals, on the secular principle that animals should not be killed—the law was also directly targeting one kind of religious practice. Its purpose, in other words, was not only *not* secular but antireligious as well.

Unanimous decisions are generally met with rejoicing by both the public and the legal community because such decisions seemingly "settle" matters, at least for a time. By the same reasoning, therefore, split decisions, especially if they are 5–4 or 6–3, suggesting not a lone holdout but a profoundly divided Court, imply very "unsettled" matters. They suggest legal disagreement over not just the substantive issues in a case but also over how to arrive at a decision—in the present instance, how to determine whether a governmental purpose is secular or not. It is hardly surprising that issues such as abortion, euthanasia, and homosexuality—all surrounded by past, present, and proposed legislation—yield divided positions among judges and the public alike.

An Aside

The division in the Court over conscience has a parallel in another long-standing philosophic division in that body: how active the Court should be in overturning the actions of the other two branches of government, especially the legislative branch. Those who advocate the "passive virtue" of inactivity tend to be found among the accommodationists, while activists tend to be found among the separationists. This correlation, of course, makes sense. If a majority, according to the first view, acting through elected representatives in a legislature, strongly desires a certain outcome, the Court should be loath to intervene unless that outcome directly contradicts the Constitution. According to the other view, the role of the judicial branch is precisely to measure the constitutionality of legislation and then outlaw those enactments not measuring up. As Justice Jackson declared so eloquently in the 1943 flag salute case (also quoted in chapter 3), the Bill of Rights was meant "to withdraw certain subjects from the vicissitudes of political controversy . . . beyond the reach of majorities and officials. . . . [F]undamental rights may not be submitted to vote." Activists regard it their duty to be watchdogs on behalf of those "fundamental rights."

This division between passive and active is further overlaid with the correlative "states' rights" issue: Disagreement exists over what powers are possessed by the federal government and what powers are retained by the individual states. Even activist judges, if they have an expanded conception of states' rights, will be less inclined to be active on issues they see as properly settled at the state level.

The Narrative Resumes

I have been arguing throughout this chapter that, once "conscience" came to enjoy the free-exercise protection given to "religion," it would follow that government actions that impose on conscience are unconstitutional unless compelling reasons exist for those impositions. We have now seen that judging "compellingness" is, in principle, not a problem but that a second requirement—that government regulations imposing on conscience must have a secular purpose—proves to be problematic in principle. Virtually all the cases discussed in chapter 4 were decided by split votes, most of them (if from the U.S. Supreme Court) by votes of 5–4, and the line of division remains constant, even with some change of Court personnel. Inasmuch as philosophic divisions in the Supreme Court change slowly, we can expect the current split on this issue of secular purpose to be maintained in some fashion for some time to come. Only if agreement can be reached on how to determine the secularity of government regulations can we hope for something close to agreement on certain matters of conscience.

That such agreement is not likely soon can be found in the four dissenters' minority opinion in the 1985 Georgia sodomy case, *Bowers v. Hardwick.* Justice Blackmun, joined by Justices Brennan, Marshall, and Stevens, points exactly to the absence of any secular purpose to the Georgia law prohibiting sodomy:

> The assertion that "traditional Judeo-Christian values proscribe" the conduct involved . . . cannot provide an adequate justification for [Georgia's law]. . . . That certain, but by no means all, religious groups condemn the behavior at issue gives the State no license to impose their judgments on the entire citizenry. *The legitimacy of secular legislation depends instead on whether the State can advance some justification for its law beyond its conformity to religious doctrine* [emphasis added].

The majority obviously had no such secular objective, nor did it recognize an obligation to seek one out. Perhaps that is why Justice Powell later expressed doubt about his vote with the majority.

Secular vs. Religious Purposes

We turn now to how the secularity of legislative or executive purposes can be identified.

David A. J. Richards, in his book *Toleration and the Constitution,* points to what might be called "public reason" to get at this issue. Public reasons involve rational principles that give "necessary and indispensable protection to the interests of adult persons in life, bodily security and integrity, security in institutional relationships and claims arising therefrom, and the like" (1986:273). Public reasons, in other words, identify what Richards calls "neutral goods—things all persons could reasonably accept as all-purpose conditions of pursuing their aims, whatever they are" (1986:259). For Richards, therefore, laws that prohibit the sale or use of contraceptives, that outlaw all abortions or homosexual relations, are unconstitutional not because some religions have moral codes declaring these activities to be sins but because they reflect no "neutral goods" that public reason can identify.

Edward B. Foley (1993:965) also utilizes the concept of public reason, which he claims has two components, epistemological and ethical:

> The epistemological component is, essentially, the methods and conclusions of logic and science. The ethical component . . . is the fundamental idea that the interests of all persons count equally for purposes of determining their rights and duties as citizens.

For Foley also, therefore, public reason involves the employment of concepts, principles, and cause-effect relations that all persons can reasonably be expected to accept.

Kyron Huigens advocates another path to much the same end. In a 1989 law review article entitled "Science, Freedom of Conscience, and the Establishment Clause," Huigens borrows an insight from Karl Popper (1968), the philosopher of science who gave us the notion of "falsifiability." "Popper's key insight," Huigens writes, "was to notice that scientific experiments are persuasive, not when they verify hypotheses, but when there is a substantial risk that they will have the opposite effect: falsification" (1989:96). Huigens would apply the falsifiability test to governmental actions and declare invalid under the Establishment Clause any actions having the "effect of advancing belief not falsifiable in principle" (1989:67).

Huigens's proposal may seem radical to some, but it conforms nicely to my argument. The strong separationist position involved in his proposal views the decisions in *Engel v. Vitale* (outlawing school prayer), *Abington Township v. Schempp* (outlawing school Bible reading), *Epperson v. Arkansas* (permitting the teaching of evolution), *Stone v. Graham* (outlawing the posting of the Ten Commandments), and all other cases involving religion in the public schools as fundamentally decisions that involve the *protection of conscience*. All these cases bar government from "advancing dogmatic belief, not because dogma is the product of an established church or because it might lead to persecution but for reasons having to do with dogma itself" (Huigens's 1989:90). In other words, dogma by definition is not falsifiable and therefore, for establishment reasons, cannot be advanced by the state.

Huigens's proposal goes considerably beyond any accommodationist position. In fact, "accommodation" of religion *as such* would disappear under his scheme, allowing for no governmental benefits to religion except those *required* by the Free Exercise Clause. Thus parochial schools would receive police and fire protection; to deny such protection would burden the free-exercise rights of parochial school students and their parents. But tax-supported bus transportation (*Everson,* 1947) would not be allowed, since the state should not assist in the promulgation of sectarian dogma. Similarly, tax-supported military chaplains are constitutional because many military personnel, away from home, are otherwise unable freely to exercise their religious rights. The legislative chaplain in the Nebraska Legislature, on the other hand, would be disallowed, contrary to *Marsh v. Chambers* (1983), because it makes the state the sponsor of a promulgator of dogma.

Huigens revisits the creation versus evolution cases (*Epperson v. Arkansas,* 1968; *Edwards v. Aguillard,* 1987) to illustrate his falsifiability principle. Any proposal to have public schools teach creationism (or creation science) is unconstitutional, not because a possibility exists that such teaching would become an "establishment" but simply because—unlike evolutionary theory, which offers falsifiable propositions—creation theory offers only immutable-truth dogma. For public schools to teach creationism, then, is to have the state use its power to assault the freedom of conscience. For the state to use its "power to inculcate, strengthen, or perpetuate belief not falsifiable in principle violates deeply held convictions about the state, belief, and the injunction to use others as ends, not means" (Huigens 1989:138–39). Read one way, this proposal appears hostile to religion; read another way, it gives priority precisely to religious liberty—it requires the state to give a wide berth to the free exercise of conscience.

Sacred Purpose
as a Residual Category

It is notable that in the several methods just reviewed for determining what is religious or secular for Establishment Clause purposes—and thus what is and is not constitutional—religion is essentially a residual category. That is, the decisive distinction involves finding what is "secular," with all else being "religious" in the eyes of the law. This makes for some surprising outcomes, of course, because much that is nonsecular is not, in the ordinary sense, religious. We saw this in chapter 4 in the vivid example of Justice Stevens's dissent in *Webster,* the 1989 Missouri abortion decision. The preamble portion of the Missouri legislative bill declared that the life of each human being begins at conception. That the preamble, wrote Stevens, happens to coincide with the tenets of one or another religion is not what disqualifies it. Rather, only if the state had a *secular* purpose in adopting the preamble would that part of the bill be constitutional. Stevens could find no secular purpose and held therefore that the preamble of the Missouri bill violates the Establishment Clause.

It bears repeating, too, that Justice Stevens is not arguing that life does *not* begin at conception, for that statement, like its opposite, also has no secular purpose. And that is exactly the point; since no known reliable and valid way exists to determine just when "life" begins, people are allowed—up until fetal viability *is* determined—to answer the question however they wish.

What is the dividing line between the two beliefs—one dealing with fetal viability, which all persons are expected to accept, and the other, dealing with the origin of life, which persons are free to answer as they choose? The best answer to this question I have encountered is Peter S. Wenz's *Abortion Rights as Religious Freedom.* His book's argument (coincident with my own) is that up until the time of fetal viability—which itself is subject to change, of course, by technological advance—a woman must, based on her free exercise of conscience, have a right to terminate her pregnancy. Wenz thus devotes a great amount of attention to this issue of the dividing line between the two kinds of belief, secular and religious. Like the authors already reviewed on this issue, Wenz defines as religious any beliefs that are not secular. Unlike secular beliefs, Wenz says (1992:136), religious beliefs

cannot be established solely by appeals to generally accepted methods of coming to know what is true and right. This is the epistemological standard for distinguishing religious from secular belief. Additionally, religious beliefs are those on which agreement is unnecessary for the co-operation required to sustain our society. They are matters on which people sharing our current way of life can agree permanently to disagree. They are not among the threads needed to hold our social fabric together.

The epistemological standard is the standard Huigens called falsifiability. It is scientific in the sense of employing normal canons of reason and evidence. Secular beliefs, in this light, do not in fact have to obtain 100 percent agreement, but at least in principle they could.

Beliefs judged to be religious by the fact that differing positions, even contradictory positions, on those beliefs need not be disruptive of social life represent a quite different category. Included are some obvious instances, such as the capacity of the unitarian, trinitarian, and atheist to live together in harmony if they choose to do so; their dogmatic differences need not interfere in their interactions. The fact that quarrels over religious beliefs *do* occur does nothing to disqualify that statement.

In sharp contrast are those beliefs about matters for which agreement *is* necessary for a smoothly functioning society. They are therefore secular beliefs. These range from seemingly simple beliefs (which side of the road to drive on) that nobody claims are religious rather than secular, to those beliefs whose origins and/or legitimation can be found in religion, such as beliefs about the immorality of murder, robbery, battery, and so on. Many of us, of course, might regard these kinds of beliefs to be religious, and in one sense they are—for those persons who conceive of their own beliefs about morality as rooted in their religion. From the legal standpoint, however, whether these beliefs are regarded by persons as rooted in their religion is immaterial; society expects people to behave in accordance with these beliefs anyway, as necessary for a stable society. This category of secular belief thus can create confusion.

American society, it might be said, has struggled over the question of how to inculcate beliefs of this second kind without getting them entangled with religious establishment. That entanglement is what underlay the decision in *Stone v. Graham* (1980), which ruled unconstitutional Kentucky's law requiring the posting of the Ten Commandments in every public school classroom. The posters themselves included a disclaimer: "The secular application of the Ten Commandments is clearly seen in its adoption as the fundamental legal code of Western Civilization and the Common Law of the United States." Perhaps, therefore, had only the last six commandments—regarding honoring parents, murder, adultery, stealing, lying, and coveting—been posted, the Supreme Court might have reached a different verdict. But also posted were the first four commandments: to remember the Sabbath, not to honor other gods, not to make graven images, and not to take God's name in vain. While posting the last six might be said to have a secular purpose, the first four could not, and therefore they are religious beliefs, promulgation of which reflects a religious purpose.

Judging from press reports, Americans generally are alarmed over our society's failure to instill a firm moral foundation into its young people. The Supreme Court's many decisions that rule out the advocacy of religion in the public schools are seen by accommodationists as misguided; granted, they say, all religious perspectives should be tolerated, but not to the point of excluding all moral education. Separationists respond by pointing out the unintended intolerant consequences of couching moral education in religious language. Instead, these separationists say, moral education can and should serve a secular purpose, a purpose all persons can hold. When that purpose is conceived as protecting the inherent consciences in all of us—however they might be articulated religiously outside of state contexts—then and only then does the "liberal principle of tolerance" become the "radical principle of liberty." The Court has made it clear that teaching *about* religion is acceptable, even necessary, for a well-rounded education; from a separationist perspective it should also approve of the teaching of values that lie behind or under all religions. Certainly it is incorrect to say that the society honoring religious liberty in this way is a society where "anything goes."

Conclusion

In raising this issue—whether and how a society may inculcate values and beliefs about those values without violating the free exercise of conscience on the one hand and the prohibition of religious establishment on the other—I come to the end of chapter 5 and point to the substance of chapter 6. People clearly have certain rights of conscience that cannot be assaulted, while the state has certain requirements that may assault certain consciences. In the ideal society these conflicts will be minimized, to the degree that individual consciences and the state's requirements coincide—to the degree, in other words, that a moral code is shared irrespective of religious doctrinal differences. Some observers have labeled this code a "civil religion," on the grounds that, in dealing more with morality than doctrine, it might be a code for all citizens. I prefer other labels for this code, as will be seen, but the subject matter of civil religion, whatever it is called, is where we turn next.

6

The Religion behind the Constitution

In the Introduction I promised that my final chapter would discuss the religion *behind* the Constitution. This is an issue of more than casual interest. One looks to Supreme Court decisions, chiefly those in the realm of church and state, to discern what the Constitution's interpreters claim the Constitution says *about* religion. And one looks at the substance of the document itself, along with those decisions, to infer what might be called the religion *of* the Constitution. In addition to these two perspectives, however, one can detect a third constitutional perspective: what Mark DeWolfe Howe called the Constitution's "attitude towards religion," an attitude, he said, that is "predominantly Protestant in spirit."

I suggest that this attitude can be imagined as "behind" the Constitution, in the same sense I believe John Mansfield means when he says (1984:856), "The Constitution embodies a particular view of human nature, human destiny, and the meaning of life. It is not neutral in regard to these matters." That the Constitution has a "particular view" does not mean that it contains a blueprint, an endpoint for all those governed by it. As Kyron Huigens states, "A constitution having such an object would place citizens in the service of the idea and so infringe on individual autonomy" (1989:116). And surely individual autonomy—the sanctity of conscience—is the central idea behind the Constitution, especially the Bill of Rights. But to speak of the "religion" behind the Constitution does imply a certain taken-for-granted status—a transcendent status, if you will. It suggests the conception of a "just life" and thus a "just society," capable of nourishing its citizens.

This is a conception that might be called "religious," even if its roots are more Aristotelian than Christian. And it is the failure to recognize this religion behind the Constitution that leads misguided souls to charge an American society endeavoring to live up to it with being "secular," "materialist," "relativist," or "Godless." The Founders recognized that the Puritan rendition of a just society was but one of many such renditions, and subsequent interpreters of their constitutional handiwork have broadened that recognition. But it does not follow that the result is a nonreligious viewpoint.

Take, for example, the reaction of syndicated columnist Cal Thomas, upon learning that Pope John Paul II had declared evolutionary theory to be "more than just a hypothesis." Committed as he is to a biblical rendition of the issue, Thomas leaps to a silly nonsequitur:

> If God . . . does not exist, and if man is not made in his image, on what basis do we appeal to a racist who wants to deny blacks equal opportunity? If man is an evolutionary accident, why pressure the Chinese over human rights abuses? Having surrendered to evolutionary theorists, the pope cannot credibly defend other doctrinal issues—such as the virgin birth, the deity of Jesus, his bodily resurrection and our salvation—because the same book that says God created the world and everything in it out of nothing also testifies to these other things. (*Los Angeles Times,* October 29, 1996)

Such silly nonsequiturs as these, I submit, the Founders meant to forestall.

The "particular view" of the United States Constitution is, from this standpoint, therefore, most certainly *not* fundamentalist Christian but is fundamentally the recognition and protection of conscience. "Human nature, human destiny, and the meaning of life," to use Mansfield's phrase, are concerns involving individuals' consciences. Another obvious alternative "particular view," for example, would have been the recognition and protection not of individual autonomy and conscience but that of various groups' authority *over* individuals. Almost from the beginning of the nation, however—certainly since Alexis de Tocqueville in 1848—the powerful forces pushing toward ever greater individualism in American life have been seen not simply as the result of urbanization and industrialization and the like but as forces importantly aided—indeed, in some sense dictated—by the implications of what the Constitution says about the rights of conscience. It is this emphasis on individualism, combined with the view that conscience is not license but a sacred obligation to be righteous, that gives the Constitution its Protestant spirit (perhaps, better, its protestant spirit).

This situation leaves the U.S. Constitution contending with the same dilemma that faces Protestant and all post-Enlightenment religion: the conflict between the authority of the group (at whatever level) and the authority of the individual conscience. If, theologically, every person is responsible for his or her own salvation (which is the case in Arminian Protestantism especially), on what basis may the group interfere with this responsibility? Of course it must interfere, as we have noted repeatedly. But with what justification? Stanley Ingber (1989:285) identifies this dilemma nicely:

> If the Constitution is to have any significance, all conflicting ideologies must defer to it and to those laws promulgated according to its mandates. However, there is one qualification to this general thesis: Religious conscience must be distinguished. An essential incompatibility exists between the potential absolution of religion and the individualistic premises of liberal political theory. . . . The religion clauses represent an acknowledgment of pre-Enlightenment beliefs and a realization that for many there are duties or obligations that precede those made by human beings.

I want to argue here that the justification for interfering with individual consciences is, paradoxically, an outgrowth of the same ideology that accords primacy to those individual consciences. The paradox, however, requires a distinction between the conscience in private and the conscience in public. Put another way, the authority of conscience in private is maintained by curtailing the authority of conscience in public. The result, of course, gives rise to a complicated tension, a tension I hope this chapter will help explain.

Religion and Conscience

A necessary first distinction must be drawn between religion and conscience. Not surprisingly, we are aided by Émile Durkheim in his monumental *The Elementary Forms of Religious Life*. He writes:

A society is not constituted simply by the mass of individuals who comprise it, the ground they occupy, the things they use, or the movements they make, but above all by the idea it has of itself. And there is no doubt that society sometimes hesitates over the manner in which it must conceive itself. It feels pulled in all directions. When such conflicts break out, they are not between the ideal and reality but between different ideals, between the ideal of yesterday and that of today, between the ideal that has the authority of tradition and one that is only coming into being. (Émile Durkheim, 1995[1912]:425)

Without doubt, among the conflicting ideals found in late-twentieth-century America is one concerning the proper role of religion in public life. One ideal harkens back to a time when religion's public authority was commonplace, while a competing ideal holds out the promise of greater religious liberty that can exist only by curtailing religion's public authority.

Underlying this conflict are two important but subtle differences between the two ideals. This first ideal conceives of religion and conscience as nearly identical, while the second ideal conceives of religion and conscience as analytically separate (though conceding that the two frequently overlap empirically).

Relatedly, the first ideal imagines that conscience emerges out of religion and therefore is necessarily articulated in religious language. The second ideal imagines religion, admittedly the language many persons use to express conscience, not as prior to but coming out of conscience. The first ideal therefore has trouble conceiving of a conscience not clothed in religious garb, while the second ideal, conceiving of conscience as anterior to religion, sees conscience amenable to expression in a variety of languages.

We have seen the conflict between these two ideals significantly revealed in court decisions, especially in the majority and minority opinions of cases involving narrow votes. Many of these cases fall into the category of church-state issues, but as we saw, particularly in chapter 4, other cases involving conscience arise outside the church-state context. That this is so is explained by the fact that in modern societies *religion is not the only language through which conscience is expressed.* Even if it were once the case, that situation has been irreversibly altered in modern plu-ralistic societies.

Émile Durkheim made this observation a century ago. In his masterful study of nineteenth-century suicide, Durkheim noted that suicide was less frequent among those persons whose consciences were bound up in morally compelling groups, including religious groups, Roman Catholic more so than Protestant. He also noted, however, that such morally com-pelling groups were on the decline. "Unless the great societies of today helplessly crumble and we return to the little social groups of long ago," he wrote, "religion will no longer be able to exert very deep or wide sway over consciences" (1951[1897]:375).

While one must agree with Durkheim on this score, one must also recog-nize that the thesis he advances is complex. Durkheim himself devoted all his scholarly energy to thinking about this matter, even to the point of seem-ing self-contradiction. Thus in *Sociology and Philosophy* (1953[1924]:71) he wrote that "it is impossible to imagine that morality should entirely sever its unbroken historical association with religion without ceasing to be itself. . . . Morality would no longer be morality if it had no element of religion."

Should we find contradiction here? Is Durkheim claiming: (a) that reli-gion and conscience are becoming separated, but (b) then morality will no longer exist? I think not and would claim that the argument I have been lay-ing out helps explain why. Consider Durkheim's statement from *Suicide* that "religion will no longer be able to exert . . . sway over consciences." Surely "religion" here refers to the church as a morally compelling group. Durkheim was noting that churches were losing their "little social group" character. Consider next his statement, "Morality would no longer be morality if it had no element of religion." Just as surely, Durkheim means here by "religion" not the church but "conscience," or that component of the self that is regarded as sacred and thus unquestioned. He was noting that the very concept of morality implies an element of unquestioned—that is, sacred—authority.

In the debate, then, about whether and how "religion" should play a role in public affairs, some are disagreeing over the question of what role the *church* should play, while others are disagreeing over the role of *conscience*. Put another way, for some the issue of religion in public affairs refers *only* to religion in the "church" sense, while for others it refers *also* to religion in the "conscience" sense. About this debate, two things seem obvious from the Supreme Court decisions we have reviewed: (1) The role of conscience is being more broadly recognized and acknowledged in the public arena (the lesson chiefly of chapter 3), and (2) the church is therefore playing a declining authoritative role in the public arena (the lesson chiefly of chapter 4). So, while religion in one sense is disappearing from public affairs, religion in another sense is increasingly apparent in those matters. These changes can be observed, however, only if "religion" and "conscience" are seen as analytically separate.

Moreover, as I have contended at several points along the way, the dynamic of this separation is structural in character; it emerges involuntarily out of prior actions, however long the process may take. This means that, whatever may be the case in any present-day empirical instance of church and/or conscientious involvement in public affairs, the likely *direction* of change is predictable.

An Example

This point can be illustrated by quoting from a letter to the editor of the *Los Angeles Times* (April 2, 1996). The writer, a man, is objecting to a column by syndicated columnist Ellen Goodman in which she says that "it's become harder and harder to muster a compelling or even logical case against same-sex marriages." The letter writer responds this way:

> The most thoughtful advocates of same-sex marriages make consent the basis for morality and therefore legality; but, as an enlightened people, are we not obliged to ask why? If the only basis for morality is consent, then it follows that incestuous relationships (and perhaps even "marriages"), so long as the father and daughter or mother and son "consent," are to be afforded the same rights and privileges as traditional families. All of us should be struck by this, and realize that something is missing

here: the only legitimate ground for morality, the "laws of nature and of nature's God." By denying a higher authority as the ground of morality, morality becomes anything we want it to be—and once a free people embrace this moral relativism, they cannot long endure.

Several points might be made. Here are three.

First, Ellen Goodman acknowledges that any "compelling case" against same-sex marriage grows ever more remote. That some persons have religious objections is obvious, she implies, but—in the words of chapter 5— no "public reason," no "falsifiable" argument, no "secular purpose" can be found to justify laws that establish one conscientious position (opposition to same-sex marriage) at the expense of another conscientious position (favoring same-sex marriage).

Second, the letter writer claims that those favoring same-sex marriage regard mere consent as the basis of morality, implying that logically, therefore, in such a scheme *any* action that persons consent to would be permissible and offering incest as an extreme example. But is it not reasonable to imagine one or more "public reasons," "falsifiable" arguments, or "secular purposes" that justify making incest illegal?

Finally, third, the letter writer claims that advocates of same-sex marriage "deny a higher authority as the ground of morality," even as he invokes the "laws of nature and of nature's God," not realizing that both assertions are made without any evidence. Unable to imagine a conscientious basis for same-sex marriage, the letter writer is equally unable to imagine that the phrase "nature's God" might mean quite different things to different people and thus carries no public authority. If he naively takes "nature's God" to be the God he understands through an infallible Bible, he can be faulted for not knowing the rules of public debate in a religiously plural society. If, on the other hand, by "nature's God" he means something akin to Jefferson's conception, then the letter writer must be prepared to offer evidence as to *why* same-sex marriage violates nature—evidence, moreover, that must be either empirically or rationally understandable to all.

Now it is clear that, with the possible exception of the case brewing in Hawaii, same-sex marriage is, as of this writing, not legal in the United

States. That is the current empirical situation. But if one were to wager on what the situation will be ten or fifty years from now, which of two possible outcomes seems to be the more likely: (1) widespread recognition of same-sex marital bonds, whatever they be called, or (2) return of oppressive laws and public scorn aimed at driving homosexual persons back into the closet? My point, remember, is not that the dynamics at issue here are inevitable by a certain date but only that they dictate the direction of change. I believe the direction to be the increased recognition of conscience as religion or the separation of "religion" and "conscience"; same-sex marriage will be seen as an issue of "conscience"; and the radical principle of religious liberty will increase another notch.

It is tempting to say, with Garry Wills, that this direction of change was determined a long time ago. Wills (1990:352) writes about Roger Williams and the Rhode Island colony:

> There is something inadvertent about much of Williams's achievement. He cared most about leading a reformed church, and could never form such a thing. He cared comparatively little about a secular state, yet that is what he set up. The tolerating state was only a means, in his mind, to serve the end of true religion. . . . The process by which those zealous for religion separated it from government presented in microcosm the process that would be worked out in America over the next centuries.

Or, as Steve Bruce summarizes (1994:240):

> What is characteristic of most modern societies is the development of a polity and a culture that minimizes . . . conflicts by requiring that considerable freedom . . . in the private sphere be matched by restraint of particularism in the public sphere.

This means, as Charles Frankel perceptively stated four decades ago (1956:83), that unity

> in a liberal society does not come from integrating ultimate values. It comes from organizing secular institutions in such a way that men's "ultimate" values—their consciences, their sense of the meaning of life, their personal dignity—do not become elements of public conflict.

One might well assume that, to the degree this arrangement is carried out, those "secular institutions" doing the task may themselves acquire "ultimate" value. It should be clear that I regard judicial institutions in exactly this way—expressing the "religion" behind the Constitution.

Is, Then, the Public Square Naked?

In his otherwise admirable book *Religion in American Life,* James Reichley offers an easily misunderstood scheme for characterizing the value systems of societies. Every person or society, he says, gives primacy to one (or a combination) of three value sources: the self, the group, and/or the transcendent (1985:chap. 2). What Reichley fails to note, however, is that while true commitment to the values of the self or the group is, in principle, verifiable by others, commitment to transcendent values is, in principle, *nonverifiable.* Of course, customs and conventions come into existence, conformity with which serve for many people as signs of commitment to a transcendent realm, but such "verification" is convincing only to those sharing a belief in the validity of those customs and conventions. That can be precarious.

Historically, therefore, this sharing in the verification process was rendered less volatile because the state, in collaboration with the church, established the customs and conventions in law. A priest was thought to exercise transcendent authority because the state joined the church in declaring that authority to be transcendent. Thus, *in a social sense,* the transcendent cannot, *by itself,* be a source of value; it must be *paired* with the self, the group, or both, because the self and/or group is needed to articulate the transcendent.

In most modern societies, however, only vestiges of an "established" church remain, as persons are free to ignore the transcendent realm altogether, just as they are free to join with others in defining what customs and conventions will be regarded *by them* as indicative of a transcendental connection. Persons may even, on their own, regard their own experiences as having transcendental meaning, which is tantamount to the situation found in some conscientious objection cases, as we noted in chapter 3. Indeed, as the 1965 *Seeger* case and the 1970 *Welsh* case made clear, courts are now willing to honor a conscientious ("transcendent") claim even if the claimant is not part of any group sharing that claim, and even if the individual claim is not made in ordinary religious language.

It is difficult to see the "public square" as "naked," therefore, just because people are free to put forward their claims in language of their own choosing. But precisely because of that freedom, they cannot expect their claims to be honored without offering reasons that in principle make sense to everyone. (This was the burden of the argument advanced in chapter 5 about judging claims of conscience.)

It is odd, therefore, to argue, as Richard John Neuhaus does, that "a public ethic cannot be reestablished unless it is informed by religiously grounded values" (1984:21), because more conscientious claims *are* being publicly recognized. And it is astounding that he later insists that "an atheist can be a citizen, but he cannot be a good citizen" (1992:207). So astounding is this second argument that we must ask for its basis. Neuhaus tells us (1992:307):

> A good citizen does more than abide by the laws. A good citizen is able to give an account, a morally compelling account, of the regime of which he is part. He is able to justify its defense against its enemies, and to recommend its virtues to citizens of the next generation. . . . Reasons must be given, reasons whose authority is drawn from that which is higher than the self and is not the self's creation, from that to which the self is ultimately obliged.

Who would not accept these criteria as befitting a good citizen? But how can it be that only "theists" qualify? Nothing in the conscientious objector cases, for example, suggests that Seeger and Welsh imagined their pacifist obligation to be self-created.

I would contend, therefore, that the public square is not naked in the sense in which Neuhaus and others use that phrase. *Some* language, as has been said, must be spoken there. The question is whether, when the language of conscience is spoken, it is recognized for what it is—"religious."

Bewailing the naked public square, as Neuhaus (1984), Carter (1993), and Thiemann (1996) do, amounts to an objection to some languages of conscience that are being used, as well as a complaint that the language of conscience they would prefer—a conventionally religious language that once had authority—is now inappropriate unless it is translatable into terms understandable by all.

A Role for Churches in Public Affairs

Does the modern "public square" require that the church stay out? Most assuredly not. Many who might want the church to stay out base their position, ironically, on the same fallacy held by those who see the square as "naked." That fallacy revolves around the issue of so-called "privatized" religion.

It has become standard wisdom in the sociology of religion, and in those who borrow—sometimes uncritically—the sociology of religion's findings, to imagine that the conditions of modern, religiously plural societies push religion into a closet and then lock the door. That, however, is not quite the correct formulation. Rather, what gets pushed into the closet is the *authority* of religion, its capacity to give orders *on its own terms in public*. In private it can be as authoritative as its followers allow.

Nothing, however, stands in the way of religion's efforts to persuade, in those terms that are acceptable (or should be acceptable) to all, the terms reviewed in chapter 5 in the discussion about judging the claims of conscience. Can religion offer *public* reasons, *falsifiable* arguments, or *secular* purposes? If so, religion is as welcome as any other participant in the public square. As José Casanova puts it (1994:223, 233):

> [W]hichever position . . . it takes, the church will have to justify it through open, public, rational discourse in the public sphere of civil society. . . . [O]nly a religion which has incorporated as its own the central aspects of the Enlightenment critique of religion is in a position today to play a positive role in . . . the revitalization of the modern public sphere.

Religion, then, is not merely tolerated in the public square but has the liberty to pursue its objective, provided only that it recognize that, in the interests of religious liberty for all, the ground rules are secular.

As is well known, the Jesuit legal scholar John Courtney Murray struggled to find a way to harmonize the theories of Roman Catholic ecclesiastical authority with American constitutional authority. In a recent book, *John Courtney Murray and the Dilemma of Religious Toleration,* Keith J. Pavlischek summarizes Murray's conclusion this way (1994:217):

> Murray knew that religious liberty was the best bet, in fact the only bet, given the sociopolitical conditions of modernity. . . . But he was also . . . aware that the type of secularized state he advocated, one that was liberated from the directions of an ecclesiastical hierarchy, could all too easily slide down the slippery slope to a secularist state devoid of all spiritual values.

Had Murray come to see religion as conscience as well as religion as church, he perhaps might have perceived that true religious liberty leads not to a secularist state devoid of spiritual values but to a secularist state of vibrantly contending spiritual values, reflecting convictions of conscience deeply held.

Admittedly, this position is easier to state than to live with. The Second Vatican Council's document on religious freedom, *Dignitatis Humanae,* itself importantly inspired by Father Murray, stirringly claimed that the Church no longer seeks recognition from the state as the true Church. Moreover, the grounds for this "inviolable constitutional right to [religious] freedom," the Council declared, are found in "the dignity of the human individual" (Burtchaell 1991:119). Another contributor to the volume containing this optimistic summary, however (Laishley 1991:224), states that

> the tensions created in the Council between the legitimate claims of theological thought and those of executive (hierarchic) power have given rise to much unfinished business. On the one hand, there are the conciliar expressions of rights of conscience and religious liberty . . . and on the other, there is a backlog of institutional theory . . . which radically subordinates critical reflection to its own executive power claiming to be *the* magisterium, the sole source of authentic teaching and rule.

Obviously, the transformation from the "liberal principle of toleration" to the "radical principle of liberty" in Roman Catholic thought is not altogether unambiguous, but then neither is that transformation unambiguous in American culture.

The Religion
behind the Constitution

It has been said many times that the Bible does not unite Christians but instead is the one thing Christians most often fight over. The same can be said about the U.S. Constitution and American citizens: What the Constitution does or does not permit, does or does not demand, is one of the things Americans quarrel over.

Various discussions of a possible American "civil religion" have often pointed to the U.S. Constitution as a central symbol of this civil religion, asserting—sometimes only implicitly—that it (along with such obvious other symbols as Washington's monuments, the flag, and so on) unite the American public. In one sense, of course, this assertion is correct if it means that most Americans attach a common meaning to those symbols. In this respect, however, the Constitution is analogous not to the Bible for Christians but to the Cross, which, as a Christian symbol, probably has a fairly uniform meaning. Such a symbolic role reflects what at the opening of this chapter I called the religion *of* the Constitution, not the religion *behind* the Constitution. Pursuant to the Bible analogy, when Christians quarrel over how to interpret that book, they are quarreling over the religion behind it. Similarly, therefore, we should look for the religion behind the Constitution by observing quarrels involving the Constitution, especially its Religion Clauses. And that is what Supreme Court cases are—quarrels over constitutional interpretation. Put simply, the Court finds one side's interpretation more convincing than the other side's, and the majority decision is, in effect, an explanation of why. In principle, the losing side is expected to understand this explanation and accept it as good and true. Ideally, then, the two erstwhile opponents are, in the end, supposed to be "unified," at least in their understanding.

It is this unifying potential of the religion *behind* the Constitution, more than its symbolic role in the religion *of* the Constitution, that comes closer, in my view, to revealing a possible American civil religion. Americans are free to accept or reject the *symbolism* of the Constitution, for example, but they are not free to accept or reject its *authority*. One ceases to *be* an American citizen in any meaningful sense if one rejects the authority of the Constitution; exile or heavily insulated social isolation are the only options, the extremist militia group being a case in point.

I doubt, however, if the undeniably religious character lying behind the Constitution warrants, by itself, the label "civil religion." The outpouring of literature inspired by Robert Bellah's seminal essay (1967), while now subsided, added up to very little increased understanding of what, in my view, is the central issue. Sanford Levinson's 1988 term "constitutional faith" is a more accurate labeling of that issue. (See also Hammond 1989 for my comments on Levinson's insightful book with that title.) Conceiving of the religion behind the Constitution in this one-dimensional way allows for variation in people's *symbolic* expression of their sacred obligation as citizens. It has been the obvious lack of consensus on such symbolism that kept discussions of civil religion from staying on track. For this reason, I have suggested that instead of "civil religion" — which invites the question "Do you believe it?" — use be made of a term such as "legitimating myth" — which invites the question "How do you understand it?" The fact is the American people understand it in a variety of ways, thus making "civil religion" an inaccurate label and a source of needless dispute. Still, if all Americans are expected to "believe" in the authority of the Constitution, is it not obvious that *some* justification should be available?

Can the Religion behind the Constitution Be Taught?

In posing the rhetorical question of whether the religion behind the Constitution can be taught, I am not asking whether it is *capable* of being taught. As with any other perspective or point of view or theory, I presume the answer is that it can, at least as readily as the multiplication table, or the doctrine of the separation of powers, or the twelve-tone scale.

What I am addressing in this final section is the question of whether, in communicating the religion behind the Constitution, say, to students in public schools, teachers would be violating the Religion Clauses of the First Amendment. The answer, I think, is this: If, by "the religion behind the Constitution," is meant what was just discussed as "constitutional faith," then no violation of the Religion Clauses occurs. If, however, by that phrase is meant "legitimating myth," then imposing a single interpretation on how and why Americans have the Constitution they have would be a violation.

Here is my reasoning. The Preamble of the U.S. Constitution itself identifies the goals for which it was "ordained" and "established." These goals include the formation of a "more perfect Union," the establishment of "Justice," the insuring of "domestic Tranquillity," and so forth. The degree to which the provisions of the Constitution (including the Bill of Rights) *succeed* in reaching those goals is certainly debatable, but whether the writers and adopters of those provisions had *faith* in their endeavor seems beyond debate. The goals they specified were not arbitrarily selected but arose out of a certain conception of humankind, a conception of persons with certain inalienable rights as individuals "endowed" by a "Creator." James Madison at least was comfortable using "conscience" to label this inviolate core of each person, but, whatever the label, the conception seems clearly more profound than mere consent, more compelling than a self-invention. That conception, I would say, can and should be taught in public school.

On that basis, and at a level appropriate to students' age, students could be offered, for example, a rationale for practicing compassion and respect toward others. They could be told with authority that lying and cheating are violations of conscience. Empathy, reconciliation, and equality could be held up as values, not because the majority approves, and not because one or more religions preach these values but because of the faith and belief that the just society requires its citizens to hold those values.

In the many discussions of whether and how religion may be taught in the public schools, therefore, those sharing the viewpoint I present here should not shy away from the kind of transcendence underlying their claims. They are religious, if by religion is meant conscience. They are secular, if by religion is meant a restrictive language of conscience.

Conclusion

Is the religion behind the Constitution "predominantly Protestant in spirit," as Mark DeWolfe Howe claimed? Yes, but only in a certain sense. Borrowing again from George Marsden's history of the American university (1994:5):

> Ironically . . . Protestant universalism . . . was one of the forces that eventually contributed to the virtual exclusion of religious perspectives from the most influential centers of American intellectual life. . . . [T]he logic of the nonsectarian ideals which the Protestant establishment had successfully promoted in public life dictated that liberal Protestantism itself should be moved to the periphery to which other religious perspectives had been relegated for some time.

Marsden calls this process ironic, and indeed it is. It is ironic in the same sense of Oliver Cromwell's plea: "I beseech ye in the bowels of Christ, think that ye may be mistaken" (quoted in Hand 1952:229). It is ironic in the same sense in which Judge Learned Hand wrote of the spirit of liberty as the "spirit that is not too sure it is right" (Hand 1952:190). One must, in other words, honor the realm of conviction while simultaneously imagining that one's own convictions need revision.

As it happened in American history, Protestant universalism influenced the ironic effort to design a society that exercised authority while at the same time allowed maximum religious freedom. That freedom began surely as widespread tolerance for all religions, but just as surely that freedom is being transformed into religious liberty, including, as I have tried to show, an increasing recognition of the rights of conscience.

To believe that such liberty means only license and thus the absence of communal responsibility is folly. To be sure, attempts to articulate that responsibility must be made in a manner that protects the rights of conscience, but the Constitution, rightly understood, shows the way.

LIST OF CASES CITED

Abington Township v. Schempp (374 U.S. 203) 1963

Agostini v. Felton (97 D.A.R. 7843) 1997

Board of Education v. Minor (13 Am. R. 233) 1872

Bowers v. Hardwick (478 U.S. 186) 1985

Braunfeld v. Brown (336 U.S. 599) 1961

Cantwell v. Connecticut (310 U.S. 296) 1940

Church of the Lukumi Babalu Aye, Inc. v. City of Hialeah (508 U.S. 520) 1993

City of Boerne v. Flores (95–2074) (138 L.ED. 20624) 1997

Compassion in Dying v. State of Washington (96 Journal D.A.R. 2639) 1996

County of Allegheny et al. v. American Civil Liberties et al. (492 U.S. 573) 1989

Cruzan v. Director, Missouri Department of Health (497 U.S. 261) 1990

Edwards v. Aguillard (482 U.S. 578) 1987

Engel v. Vitale (370 U.S. 421) 1962

Epperson v. Arkansas (393 U.S. 97) 1968

Everson v. Board of Education (330 U.S. 1) 1947

Fellowship of Humanity v. County of Alameda (153 Cal. App. 2d 673) 1957

Grand Rapids School District v. Ball (473 U.S. 373) 1984

Harris v. McRae (448 U.S. 297) 1979

Jones v. Opelika (316 U.S. 594) 1942

Lee v. Weisman (505 U.S. 577) 1992

Lemon v. Kurtzman (403 U.S. 602) 1971

Marbury v. Madison (1 U.S. Cranch 137) 1803

Marsh v. Chambers (463 U.S. 783) 1983

Minersville School District v. Gobitis (310 U.S. 586) 1940

Murdock v. Pennsylvania (319 U.S. 105) 1943

Oregon Employment Division v. Smith (494 U.S. 872) 1990

Planned Parenthood v. Casey (505 U.S. 833) 1992

Reynolds v. United States (98 U.S. 145) 1879

Roe v. Wade (410 U.S. 113) 1973

Sherbert v. Verner (374 U.S. 398) 1963

Stone v. Graham (449 U.S. 39) 1980

Torcaso v. Watkins (223 MD 49) 1960

Torcaso v. Watkins (367 U.S. 488) 1961

Trans World Airlines, Inc. v. Hardison (432 U.S. 488) 1977

United States v. Ballard (322 U.S. 78) 1944

United States v. Kauten (133 F. 2d. 703) 1943

United States v. Seeger (380 U.S. 163) 1965

Vacco et al. v. Quill et al. (95–1858) (138 L.ED. 20834) 1997

Wallace v. Jaffree (472 U.S. 38) 1985

Washington et al. v. Glucksberg et al. (96–110) (138 L.ED. 20772) 1997

Watson v. Jones (80 U.S. 679) 1872

Webster v. Reproductive Health Services (492 U.S. 490) 1988

Welsh v. United States (398 U.S. 333) 1970

West Virginia State Board of Education v. Barnette (319 U.S. 624) 1943

Wisconsin v. Yoder (406 U.S. 205) 1972

BIBLIOGRAPHY

Bellah, Robert N.
1967   "Civil Religion in America." *Daedalus* (Winter).

Berman, Harold J.
1989   "The Religion Clauses of the First Amendment in Historical Perspective." In *Religion and Politics,* edited by W. Lawson Taitte, 47–73. Austin, Tex.: University of Texas Press.

Borden, Martin
1984   *Jews, Turks, and Infidels.* Chapel Hill, N.C.: University of North Carolina Press.

Bruce, Steve
1994   "The Inevitable Failure of the New Christian Right." *Sociology of Religion* 55:229–42.

Burtchaell, James T.
1991   "Religious Freedom." In *Modern Catholicism: Vatican II and After,* edited by Adrian Hastings. New York: Oxford University Press.

Carmela, Angela C.
1993   "The Religion Clauses and Acculturated Religious Conduct: Boundaries for the Regulation of Religion." In *The Role of Government in Monitoring and Regulating Religion in Public Life,* edited by James R. Wood and Derek Davis, 21–49. Waco, Tex.: J. M. Dawson Institute of Church-State Studies.

Carter, Stephen
 1993   *The Culture of Disbelief.* New York: Basic Books.

Casanova, José
 1994   *Public Religions in the Modern World.* Chicago: University of Chicago Press.

Davis, Derek
 1993   "The Courts and the Constitutional Meaning of 'Religion': A History and Critique." In *The Role of Government in Monitoring and Regulating Religion in Public Life,* edited by James R. Wood and Derek Davis, 89–119. Waco, Tex.: J. M. Dawson Institute of Church-State Studies.

Demerath, N. J., III
 1991   "Religious Capital and Capital Religions." *Daedalus* 120:21–40.

Dolbeare, Kenneth, and Phillip E. Hammond
 1971   *The School Prayer Decision.* Chicago: University of Chicago Press.

Durkheim, Émile
 [1897] *Suicide.* Edited and translated by J. A. Spaulding and G. Simpson.
 1951   Chicago: Free Press.
 [1924] *Sociology and Philosophy.* Translated by P. F. Pocock. Chicago: Free
 1953   Press.
 [1912] *The Elementary Forms of Religious Life.* Translated by Karen E.
 1995   Fields. New York: Free Press.

Dworkin, Ronald
 1993   *Life's Dominion.* New York: Alfred A. Knopf.

Eskridge, William N., Jr.
 1996   *The Case for Same-Sex Marriage.* New York: Free Press.

Finke, Roger, and Rodney Stark
 1992   *The Churching of America, 1776–1990.* New Brunswick, N.J.: Rutgers University Press.

Fitzpatrick, James K.
 1985   *God, Country, and the Supreme Court.* Chicago: Regnery Books.

Flowers, Ronald B.
1993   "Government Accommodation of Religious-Based Conscientious Objection." *Seton Hall Law Review* 24:2.
1994   *That Godless Court?* Louisville, Ky.: Westminister John Knox Press.

Foley, Edward B.
1993   "Political Liberalism and Establishment Clause Jurisprudence." *Case Western Reserve Law Review* 43:963–81.

Frankel, Charles
1956   *The Case for Modern Man.* New York: Harper & Row.

Frankel, Marvin E.
1992   "Religion in Public Life: Reasons for Minimal Access." *George Washington Law Review* 60:633–44.
1994   *Faith and Freedom.* New York: Hill & Wang.

Galanter, Marc
1966   "Religious Freedoms in the United States: A Turning Point?" *Wisconsin Law Review* 1966:217–96.

Gerth, Hans, and C. Wright Mills, ed.
1946   *From Max Weber: Essays in Sociology.* New York: Oxford University Press.

Greenawalt, Kent
1993   "The Role of Religion in a Liberal Democracy." *Journal of Church and State* 35:503–19.

Hammond, Phillip E.
1984   "The Courts and Secular Humanism." *Society* 21:11–16.
1989   "Constitutional Faith, Legitimating Myth, Civil Religion." *Law and Social Inquiry* 14:377–91.
1992   *Religion and Personal Autonomy: The Third Disestablishment in America.* Columbia, S.C.: University of South Carolina Press.

Hand, Learned
1952   *The Spirit of Liberty.* New York: Alfred A. Knopf.

Handy, Robert T.

[1971]   *A Christian America: Protestant Hopes and Historical Realities.* New
1984   York: Oxford University Press.
1991   *Undermined Establishment: Church-State Relations in America,*
         1880–1920. Princeton, N.J.: Princeton University Press.

Himmelfarb, Milton

1968   "Secular Society? A Jewish Perspective." In *Religion in America,*
         edited by William G. McLoughlin and Robert N. Bellah. Boston: Bea-
         con Press.

Howe, Mark DeWolfe

1950   "Review of Anson Phelps Stokes, Church and State in the United
         States." *Harvard Law Review* 64:170–72.
1965   *The Garden in the Wilderness.* Chicago: University of Chicago Press.

Hudson, Winthrop S., and John Corrigan

1992   *Religion in America.* 5th ed. New York: Macmillan Publishing Co.

Huigens, Kyron

1989   "Science, Freedom of Conscience, and the Establishment Clause." *Uni-*
         versity of Puget Sound Law Review 13:65–163.

Hunter, James D.

1991   *Culture Wars: The Struggle to Define America.* New York: Basic
         Books.

Ingber, Stanley

1989   "Religion or Ideology: A Needed Clarification of the Religion
         Clauses." *Stanford Law Review* 41:233–333.

Johnson, Phillip E.

1984   "Concepts and Compromise in First Amendment Religious Doctrine."
         California Law Review 72:817–46.

Jones, Richard H.

1986   "Accommodationist and Separationist Ideals in Supreme Court Estab-
         lishment Clause Decisions." *Journal of Church and State* 28:193–223.

Konvitz, Milton R.

1968   *Religious Liberty and Conscience.* New York: Viking Press.

Laishley, F. J.
1991   "Unfinished Business." In *Modern Catholicism: Vatican II and After,* edited by Adrian Hastings. New York: Oxford University Press.

Lefler, Hugh T., et al.
1973   *The History of a Southern State: North Carolina.* Chapel Hill, N.C.: University of North Carolina Press.

Lerner, Ralph
1989   "Believers and the Founders' Constitution." *This World* 26.

Levinson, Sanford
1988   *Constitutional Faith.* Princeton, N.J.: Princeton University Press.

Levy, Leonard W.
1986   *The Establishment Clause.* Chapel Hill, N.C.: University of North Carolina Press.

Lippy, Charles H.
1978   "The 1780 Massachusetts Constitution: Religious Establishment or Civil Religion?" *Journal of Church and State* 20:533–49.

Malbin, Michael J.
1978   *Religion and Politics: The Intentions of the Authors of the First Amendment.* Washington, D.C.: American Enterprise Institute.

Mansfield, John H.
1984   "The Religion Clauses of the First Amendment and the Philosophy of the Constitution." *California Law Review* 72:847–907.

Marsden, George M.
1994   *The Soul of the American University: From Protestant Establishment to Established Nonbelief.* New York: Oxford University Press.

McConnell, Michael W.
1942   "Accommodation of Religion: An Update and a Response to the Critics." *George Washington Law Review* 60:685–742.

1992   "Religious Freedom at a Crossroads." *University of Chicago Law Review* 59:115–94.

McLoughlin, William G.
1978   *Revivals, Awakenings, and Reform.* Chicago: University of Chicago Press.

Michaelsen, Robert S.
1970   *Piety in the Public School.* New York: Macmillan Publishing Co.

Moen, Matthew C.
1992   *The Transformation of the Christian Right.* Tuscaloosa, Ala.: University of Alabama Press.

Moskos, Charles C., and John Whiteclay Chambers II, ed.
1993   *The New Conscientious Objection: From Sacred to Secular Resistance.* New York: Oxford University Press.

Neuhaus, Richard John
1984   *The Naked Public Square.* Grand Rapids: Wm. B. Eerdmans Publishing Co.
1992   "Can Atheists Be Good Citizens?" In *Being Christian Today,* edited by Richard John Neuhaus and George Weigel, 295–308. Washington D.C.: Ethics and Public Policy Center.

Norman, E. R.
1968   *The Conscience of the State in North America.* London: Cambridge University Press.

Pavlischek, Keith J.
1994   *John Courtney Murray and the Dilemma of Religious Toleration.* Kirksville, Mo.: Thomas Jefferson University Press.

Pfeffer, Leo
1984   *Religion, State, and the Burger Court.* Buffalo: Prometheus Books.

Popper, Karl
1968   *The Logic of Scientific Discovery,* rev. ed. London: Hutchinson.

Rakove, Jack N.
1996   *Original Meanings.* New York: Alfred A. Knopf.

Reichley, James
1985   *Religion in American Life.* Washington, D.C.: Brookings Institution.

Richards, David A. J.
1986   *Toleration and the Constitution.* New York: Oxford University Press.

Richardson, James T.
1995 "Legal Status of Minority Religions in the United States." *Social Compass* 42:249–64.

Robbins, Thomas
1993 "The Intensification of Church-State Conflict in the United States." *Social Compass* 40:505–27.

Sherwood, Carlton
1991 *Inquisition*. Washington, D.C.: Regnery/Gateway.

Shipton, C. K.
1965 "The Locus of Authority in Colonial Massachusetts." In *Law and Authority in Colonial America,* edited by G. A. Billias. Barre, Mass.: Barre Publishers.

Smith, Steven D.
1995 *Foreordained Failure: The Quest for a Constitutional Principle of Religious Freedom*. New York: Oxford University Press.

Stone, Harlan Fiske
1919 "The Conscientious Objector." *Columbia University Quarterly* 21.

Story, Joseph
[1833] *Commentaire on the Constitution of the United States*. Boston: Hilliard,
1970 Gray & Co.; reprint New York: Da Capo Press.

Sullivan, Andrew
1995 *Virtually Normal*. New York: Alfred A. Knopf.

Sullivan, Kathleen
1992 "Religion and Liberal Democracy." *University of Chicago Law Review* 59:195–223.

Swomley, John M.
1987 *Religious Liberty and the Secular State*. Buffalo: Prometheus Books.

Thiemann, Ronald F.
1996 *Religion in Public Life*. Washington, D.C.: Georgetown University Press.

de Tocqueville, Alexis
[1848] *Democracy in America*. Translated by George Lawrence and edited by
1969   J. P. Mayer. Garden City, N.Y.: Anchor Books.

Urofsky, Melvin I.
1993   *Letting Go: Death, Dying, and the Law*. New York: Charles Scribner's
Sons.

Wallace, Anthony F. C.
1956   "Revitalization Movements." *American Anthropology* 58:264–81.

Washington, James M.
1992   "The Crisis in the Sanctity of Conscience in American Jurisprudence."
De Paul Law Review 42:11–60.

Way, H. Frank
1987   "Death of the Christian Nation: The Judiciary and Church-State Relations." *Journal of Church and State* 29:509–29.

Wenz, Peter S.
1992   *Abortion Rights as Religious Freedom*. Philadelphia: Temple University Press.

Wills, Garry
1990   *Under God: Religion and American Politics*. New York: Simon &
Schuster.

INDEX

SWAN LIBRARY
BECKER COLLEGE-LEICESTER, MA